I0813266

NOBODY'S PSYCHIC

NOBODY'S PSYCHIC

FINDING & LOSING YOURSELF

DANI LAMORTE

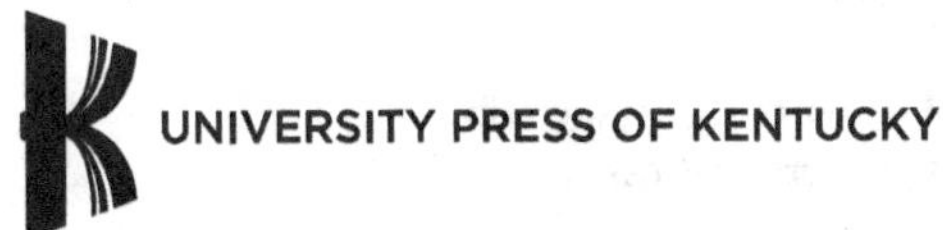

A note to the reader: This is a work of creative nonfiction, and events are portrayed to the best of the author's memory. Some passages contain sensitive material, including language that, in other contexts, is associated with homophobia. The opinions and interpretations are solely those of the author.

Published by The University Press of Kentucky, scholarly publisher for the Commonwealth, serving Bellarmine University, Berea College, Centre College of Kentucky, Eastern Kentucky University, The Filson Historical Society, Georgetown College, Kentucky Historical Society, Kentucky State University, Morehead State University, Murray State University, Northern Kentucky University, Spalding University, Transylvania University, University of Kentucky, University of Louisville, University of Pikeville, and Western Kentucky University.

Editorial and Sales Offices: The University Press of Kentucky
663 South Limestone, Lexington, Kentucky 40508-4008
www.kentuckypress.com

Cataloging-in-Publication data is available from the Library of Congress.

ISBN 978-1-9859-0281-7 (hardcover : alk. paper)
ISBN 978-1-9859-0282-4 (pbk. : alk. paper)
ISBN 978-1-9859-0284-8 (epub)
ISBN 978-1-9859-0283-1 (pdf)

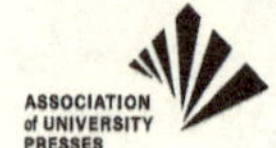

Member of the Association
of University Presses

Contents

Introduction

Swissvale, August 2023

His black paw touched the sidewalk as a gesture of learned habit. Where claws would emerge was a splay of thorns. There were other words, too: spines, glochids, needles, prickles. Our cat, then a semistray living in the converging parking lots of our Tucson apartment complex, was returning from an overnight encounter with a cactus. He bounded over the brick wall behind our apartment to access his food bowl, then did a three-leg trot into our bedroom for a daytime nap. While he slept, I used small tweezers to pull out all those cactus bits. He'd wake, push my hand away, then lick it. Then back to sleep and tweezers back to work. We like to say he got in a fight with a cactus and, in his mind, he won.

The cactus, though I was not there, may have been a prickly pear—genus *Opuntia*. In scientific taxonomy, the genus is a level of grouping that immediately precedes the "specific epithet" or species name. The species name is, sometimes, the most fine-grained identification for a plant. For instance: *Opuntia ficus-indica*, where *Opuntia* is the genus and *ficus-indica* is the species. It's a kind of *Opuntia* called *ficus-indica*. "Indian fig prickly pear," in English, unitalicized and sounding like something you can see. But *Opuntia* is lovely, with its *punt* puncturing, sliding through slippery vowels like a boot through Jell-O. So let's stick with the Latin name for the beauty of it.

It could have been an *Opuntia* who left my cat hobbling, but in the Sonoran Desert, it is hard to be sure. There's *Opuntia, Cylindropuntia, Echinocactus,* and the saguaro—in planted Latin, *Carnegia gigantea.* For better or worse, the name "Carnegie" makes me feel at home. Andrew Carnegie's genus is in the steel and cement of buildings in my home city, Pittsburgh. Harrison, my partner, and I moved from Pittsburgh to Tucson in 2015. Harrison was starting their doctoral studies. I was starting this book, only I didn't know it. What I knew acutely was that I'd left the sticky, gelatinous summers of southwestern Pennsylvania for the arid Southwest. I remember the first few hours of living in Tucson, the six-lane streets and infinite strip malls wobbling in August heat. They didn't look quite real, like film sets. If I glanced behind the facade of a Ross Dress for Less or Alvernon Optical, I thought I might see two-by-fours holding up some plywood backing. But I went through the doors and saw that the stores and the plants and the people were all real, and real to one another.

"Real" is a false cognate for the Spanish word *real,* meaning "royal." False cognates are words that look like they might mean the same thing in two languages, but they don't. For instance, the French word for "bread" looks like an English word for something more complicated to purchase—*pain.* Maybe what's real is what's royal. Real is a selection of apparitions and sensory enervations. The selection is made by someone with a sort of power to decree. It could be a real royal deciding, or a jumble-body like "Congress" imagining along the bodies of children, deciding which ones are real boys and girls. It could be a part of your mind making the decisions, splitting "what really happened" from all the stories you could tell but don't. What's real becomes the basis of what happens next, what becomes real next. What's real could be a prophetess's small-town heraldings, a man who only existed in the misspelling of his name, or a scene from *Free Willy* you've only seen in your mind. What's real can become fake too: a dusty plastic tulip standing in for windmills and spring. Royals fall from thrones, memories from our minds.

Memory's never been my strong suit, at least not the kind of memory that leads to history. Historians, and their archivist kin, try to figure out what "really happened." What "really happened" is a story with clear eyes, vision corrected, in best focus. The lighting is plain and even. As a young child, I learned from religious zealots that history is only one way to see the world. You can also come to appreciate your astigmatisms, floaters, improper attentions, and nearsightedness. Demons can wander your living room; angels, your garden shed. The name of a street can be part of a message from God, along with a dream of indigestion and the passing greeting of a Kmart cashier. You can learn to need a kind of sight into which you dissolve. What's true, what "really happened" can be a vision of the world flowing through you. There are times when I'm angry at these zealots, heartbroken by the vision of heaven they gave me. Undeniably, though, they gave me a sort of preview: What is it like to appreciate an experience inside yourself as much as you appreciate the "truth" you share with others?

"Inside yourself" can feel like a trap. Who could understand how you feel when they've not seen what you've seen? There's some truth to that, but there's also nothing to do about that. There's pleasure, too, in having a world inside you that feels like it's not completely negotiated with others. In between the horror and thrill of being an individual being is what Kaja Silverman calls "the miracle of analogy."

That's sort of a lie. *The Miracle of Analogy* is what Silverman called her book, but I think what she says in the book gets to my point. In her book, and I hope a little in this one, Silverman suggests that the most fantastic thing about photography as a technology is that it allows the things around us to disclose themselves to us. A photograph of a fake tulip becomes an iteration, a repetition, an analogy of the fake tulip. It's a kind of message from the world to us, made of photo chemicals, papers and films, lenses and lights. Analogies, things that bear striking correspondence to one another while still being different from one another, allow us to satisfy all the desires we get from the durable poverty of loneliness and the weakness of self-sufficiency.

Through analogy, the photo of the fake tulip and the fake tulip come to be part of one another. That's how the fake tulip, the living tulip, the camera, the film, and the photo print all come to become tangled together too. Plants—both the kind made of plastic and the kind made otherwise—are fantastically similar to cameras and photographs. Inside each, great power is made from the focusing of light. Early photography relied heavily on sunlight, the stuff of plants' continuance. I think of living plants and cameras as eating the sun, and the sun as eating printed photographs and polyester corsages. It's a rough nosh, to be sure, but it's also a display of love in the old Freudian way: what I want, I want inside me. I eat my desires. Sometimes we make up new organs to do this eating, like when we build industrial spinnerets that turn synthetic threads into houseplants that cannot die. We want, so badly, to be part of the life of plants that we start consuming all sorts of resources just so we might make worshipful analogies to them.

In the pages to come, I take a lot of liberty in building metaphors and analogies, because this isn't history. There are stories on these pages, but I'm not telling you what really happened as seen through a clear camera lens and pressed into new film. I'm telling you what I see when I look through memory, wishing, forgetting, and—sometimes—a refusal to look. Pittsburgh and Tucson, Tucson and the Kiskiminetas Valley, get stuck together, as do artificial lakes, filmic whales, invading trees, sounds on the tip of your tongue, and photos drowning in solar rays. Here and now, now and then, there and *maybe* aren't ever separate from one another. The idea of such separations is, to me, a vision seen by adherents of history and the archives.

I take liberty, too, in talking to you
hello, yes, you
as though you were here, wherever here might be, maybe a restaurant
I'll have the Caesar
and I'm telling you all this,
real friendly.

Good storytelling behavior, well-mannered argument, both so devoted to clear history, can only go so far into the charged interstice of a metaphor. So, I talk, a little, here and there, when I feel the story breaking down, giving up, ending up covering over what really happened inside me, even if it never really happened anywhere else.

God is one of those inside happenings. I do not believe in God as an entity, but in these pages I probe God as a psychological specter, a mental limit, an animal impossibility. If God is sacred, he's sacred as Georges Bataille defined it: something beyond utility, transformed through sacrifice into a splendor of wasted excess. In Bataille's thought, vital life takes place in the useless splurge: the sacrifice, the carnival, the orgy, the moments spent only breathing, spent idling on the very edge of what's knowable. When we know how empty we are—how fundamentally alone and meaningless we are—*that's* when something's happening. It's unbearable to have that something happening all the time, though. We have no option but to press outward and try to communicate, to break the isolation, in speech or art or building a campfire. We'd have no reason to speak if it weren't impossible.

Bataille was an atheist, but he suggested that were God to exist, he would be an entity who could bear to stay with the knowledge of his own insufficiency. Such a God would be continually burning up on the edge of what is knowable and in the awareness of his own nothingness. Like Bataille, I do not believe in such a spectacularly tortured being. A god who answers prayers, who frets about meaty beings on a flung rock, is not sacred in this way of thinking but profane—an invention we've made to serve a purpose. I understand the god I met at the age of five to be terribly purposeful.

Over centuries, Christofascism, paired with ethnonationalism and ecocide, has come to dominate the American cultural landscape, to impoverish the intellectual, emotional, and physical lives of so many. I grew up espousing these very ideologies, and so I want to tell you about the concept of God that once menaced me, that I desperately wanted to impose on others, that sometimes continues to follow me. If my anger offends, perhaps it is because my anger points to a profound disappointment—felt by myself and some readers—at what I, and so many children who grew up in fundamentalist circles, survived. As I revise this introduction, Republican political candidates are using the idea of God to meddle in the bodies of millions—denying trans health care, criminalizing abortion, and maligning all nonprocreative sexuality. History and culture, not metaphysics, separate God and religion from other areas of human inquiry: aesthetics, language, eroticism. So I respond to the god of my childhood faith, who some wish to make the god of this country, as I might respond to any oppressing force. I refuse him with fury and laughter.

To many Americans, it is still scandalous for atheists to speak directly of our convictions, to refuse to equivocate: there is no god, and we will not be beholden to the imagining of one. My atheism informs my writing on God and faith, but my atheism is also mutated by my religious upbringing. I will never know what it is to live without having believed truly, terrifyingly, obsessively. I will never know what it is to live without having sensed that something omniscient and omnipotent is trailing me, judging my every mental and physical secret. Perhaps because I know that feeling, I am ever the more committed to refusing its power, to laughing in its face, to giving God the insufficiency that—if he existed—he would require.

Detailing my religious experiences necessitates detailing the characters—the churchgoers, the pastors, the televangelists—who were alongside me. While it's possible they were experiencing something sacred, in Bataille's sense, I would argue that they were mostly communing with ordinary human feelings. At times, people I knew prayed because they truly felt they needed to speak to something outside themselves. At times, they prayed to enact a social power over others. At times, they perhaps prayed because it felt like it was really *doing something.* In this book, I open the god I knew, and his followers, to the questions that I dared not ask when I was younger.

I thought this book might be called *Of Fakes*. Say it aloud and find out, as I did, that it's not very speech-friendly. Offakes. Ovvakes. Ovakes. I played with another title too: *Nothing to See*. *Nothing to See* is easier to say, but it's a lie—but lies are analogies too. They're duplicates or dupes of what we want in the world, or want to see outside ourselves. At times, I've thought I was nothing to see. I thought I might not exist. Other times, I've wished there was nothing to see, nothing of me, nothing of you, nothing of anything anywhere. I did not want to find analogies, not even in my lies. In better times, I wonder what it is to see *nothing*. What are all those fantastic bodies without eyes—the bodies of plants, of corals, in photos and in paint—all doing? Where's the metaphor or analogy through which I might come to bridge what's inside us?

To tell you what I see, when I'm seeing nothing or many things, I have to tell you a couple stories about me. I see the way I do because I was a poor, rural, Evangelical, neurotic faggot. Unfortunately, those bits of self-description tend to magnify the pain each generates, like sounds building mutual interference in a concrete room. Maybe some of those self-descriptions are themselves built from the noise and pain. Fortunately, I taught myself a great deal of French (the language of poor, rural, Evangelical, neurotic faggots), and I know now that pain is *pain*: it's bread, it's something I can make exist outside of myself. You'll consume it, in its new form, as a way of getting some of me inside of you. Pain is a basis for analogy. I try to use it carefully in these pages, to encourage rather than mute appetite.

Julia Child says that in order to flip an omelet without a spatula, "You must have the courage of your convictions." Some things, like flipping an omelet or sharing what's inside us, are easier than they seem at times. You just have to mean to do it. Meaning to do it is the hard part, but I mean to flip the omelet that is the book, and to open all these metaphors and analogies up for you. I hope you'll mean to eat these words and find the space in between inside both of us.

I hope you'll mean to dig in.

PART I
FAKE

Tell Them Queen Anne Sent You

Swissvale, Pennsylvania, 2023

Don't offer me a lawn mower. There's no use. I won't use it I don't want it and, besides, the slope is too steep and littered with supermarket weeklies, condom wrappers, Styrofoam cups, and, I think, a bottle of piss. I didn't open it. I didn't really want to know.

My neighbor offered us a lawn mower, to me and my partner, Harrison.

"Let me know if you want to borrow my lawn mower!"

I am certain a meeting was held somewhere on the block, and all in attendance agreed to this offer. The plants growing around our house are too tall—according to her, the other neighbors, the borough code. I know they're too tall by those measures.

I keep retelling myself all the reasons to let things get tall, too tall, break-the-blades-of-the-mower tall, because if she asks, if the neighbor asks, I'll need all the reasons, and I know I'm forgetting them. So I'm repeating the reasons to myself—"ecology, the climate, soil health"—and not repeating something else:

I can't bear to be the one who cuts these lives back.

The whole time, she talks in my imagination, offers again, that machine, in my imagination. *And so, wait, I forget, wait, yes, wait, OK, stop.*

I can't hear her.

What's she saying?

What's going on here?

Here being Swissvale, Pennsylvania, a borough bordered by the city of Pittsburgh, the borough of Rankin, and the

Monongahela River. When I moved to Swissvale, I hoped its name might derive from a plucky batch of Swiss immigrants or some kind of outlandish Swiss Miss hot cocoa trivia. In fact, the borough is named for John Swisshelm, whose pre–Civil War farmstead held the land that would become a small town. In the early twentieth century, Swissvale was home to Kopp Glass as well as the Westinghouse Air Brake Company. Kopp Glass invented a red, selenium-based glass used for railroad stoplights. Westinghouse air brakes made color into action.

I suppose I broke, too, when I sensed that offer coming. The lawn mower, cutting things up, seizing up, breaking off the air coming into my lungs. Local trivia is good for making these kinds of associations and figuring out which plots of dirt have a meaning you need.

Where are we again?

Swissvale, and it doesn't matter. My apologies to our mayor, the budget, and the little red fire truck that wanders borough streets on Halloween night, chucking candy at teens. Swissvale's not real, not separate from anything around it. Then, at other times, it's real, like when the bridge closed.

The Washington Avenue Bridge was constructed in 1907—a simple jump over the train tracks below, keeping Washington Avenue contiguous between the commercial strips of Monongahela and Noble Streets. At its construction, ownership was split between Swissvale borough and the railroad company. When, inevitably, the bridge needed repairs decade after decade, each party felt the other ought to pick up the tab. Residents waited. Walkways crumbled onto the railway. *Wait.* Rainwater carried iron oxide from the bridge's struts to the soil below, making a gruesome carmine. *Wait.* The bridge closed to all motor traffic in July 2022 because of structural instability. *Wait.* It's still closed. *Wait*, still.

I hear a new bridge is coming. The railroad will pay for it. The borough will own it on their own. Until they can't afford to repair it on their own. *Wait.*

Swissvale isn't Pittsburgh. But it is when I look out my studio window and see it, the red stoplight, a quarter mile away, across the river, in the night, stopping cars I can't see in the dark. And when it turns green, they all go, and it turns out the green is too far away for me to see it where it is, in Homestead, another borough that is not Pittsburgh, but the rivers and red lights don't know that. We don't know where we are.

Pittsburgh and its adjacent boroughs are undeniably similar in ecology and topography to the small towns I'm from. They're only about an hour away from each other, Pittsburgh and that riverside cluster. We all flatten some of our vowels the same, push others up against the spitty insides of our lips. I don't remember anybody ever pointing out how we spoke in those towns, except the outlander English teacher who told us what "ain't" ain't and noted the lack of "r" in our nation's capital. Nobody ever said that we sounded like we were "from Pittsburgh" though. It wouldn't have made any sense. Pittsburgh was a city far away, glimpsed only on school field trips. Pittsburgh was full of drugs, something called "sex," and a whole bunch of sin. Our towns, I thought, didn't have much to do with that city downriver. The too-tall trees and herbs and "weeds" outside my house now and then show how wrong I was.

Queen Anne's lace flowers here and there like a garden carrot. In the marshy flows adjacent to my high school, stands of the tall white flower heads were mottled by cattails. "High school" is generous. Founded in the 1970s, Arbor Heights Christian Academy was an old house built into a hillside, sutured to a gymnasium that looked like an airplane hangar. It sat at the top of a small hill, with a matching church at the base. Both buildings were a lazy white. Architectural apathy. The path up the hill was bifurcated by a creek that crossed the religious property. Cars drove over the creek thanks to one of those things that I don't know the word for but I've seen all my life—a sort of length of big metal pipe, several feet in diameter and strong enough to hold up traffic. The pipe thing was placed in the flow of the stream and covered with dirt so that the path up the hill and the path of the water both could be continuous. Small crab apple trees were to the left of the school's front doors. Behind the school were woods, and to the left of the building, down another slope, was a big field.

The school was created in the 1970s because public schools, *secular* schools, were a problem. Nobody was praying in class anymore, and teens were doing all sorts of big-city things during school hours. Concerned Christian parents affiliated with the ugly church at the bottom of the hill decided their children needed uplift. They needed a school that taught the truth: women came from an old man's rib and not a monkey's future. I could know more about the school, tell you more, if I went back and asked.

And would you come with me? I mean, I don't want to go back alone, again, and ask them all what happened back then and then again when I was around. I won't go alone, like I do in my dreams. You gotta go, gotta wake up. Get up. Come with me and we'll ask that thing you wanted to know.

How did we get here?

I dreamed of becoming a student at that private Christian school, in the way you dream of things you'll regret getting. At the end of my sixth year of elementary school, I was terrified of the public high school so close in my future. I'd only seen it once. Big brick thing, built I don't know when. My siblings all went there, graduated from there. It was along a semicommercial road, across from a Kmart and next to a Mister Donut.

Isn't it sad when you realize people like Mister Donut aren't real? It's just a coffee shop where your dad,

sorry, my dad, unless your dad was there, too, I don't know, I wasn't there that much,

more than the high school, though,

and he goes there to eye up the teen girls who get you a vanilla frosted with sprinkles because you're very well behaved for—

sorry—I'm well behaved for a four-year-old. Maybe you were, too.

Downriver from Mister Donut were creatures whose realness was not up for debate. Demons and angels populated my eyeline. Our church preached the literal, empirical presence and agency of these otherworldly beings in day-to-day life. I saw them with my vision, some interval of sight that happens in the synaptic gaps where the mind stitches together the "what" of "What is this?" In the eyes of my church, there was nothing peculiar about these visions. The electric guitarist who played "Amazing Grace" on Sunday and worked in the glass mill on Monday had visions. So did the supermarket advertising executive who occasionally lent her contralto voice. So did the part-time accountant, full-time hoarder who sang at her pew, a semitone out of tune. We practiced seeing together and voicing our visions.

The demons, I was convinced, were coming for me at my public elementary school. They were animating bullies to kick me in the crotch, shove me on the stairs, exile me to a lunch table of my own. In recent months, they had been animating me too, moving me.

Where am I going?

It could only get worse as the demons got bigger, grew up, filled up with bricks and donuts. And there was a Mister Donut mug—white plastic with a brown lid. Nothing kept the hole in the lid closed,

so hot coffee keeps hitting my arm, and I'm walking too fast, but I've got to keep moving

My sixth-grade class was taught by Mr. F, as he quixotically insisted on being known. Tall and muscular, with hair left over from the 1980s.

"What part of speech is this?" He'd quiz the class, his middle finger pointing at the part in question, written in white chalk. In the first weeks of the school year, we students would laugh, scandalized by his means of indicating. He was young but already numb to the prepubescent wish for chaos. His face stayed still. We stopped laughing.

"What part of speech is this?" I parroted minutes later. Mr. F had left the classroom, and I felt an overwhelming urge to take his stage. I pointed like he did, first at the board, then at my classmates, each of them my little chalkboards.

"Do you know, Kevin?" I gave Kevin the finger. "How about you, Peter?"

When Mr. F returned, I was still pointing at a fellow student. Now, he pointed at me with his index finger.

"What are you doing?" The reason had left me before the words left his mouth.

After school, I played with fire on the kitchen stove. I made kindling of junk mail. A sheet of burning bill caught an updraft and floated across the kitchen, landing on the carpet of our rented house. It melted a large, circular patch of the cheap plastic flooring. It melted a smaller circular patch of the skin on my left wrist. My mother, too, wanted to know, "What are you doing?" I stared at the bubbling flooring, my blistering skin without an answer. To date, I'd been a pretty obedient kid. Good grades, nose in the teacher's bell. I did not know this finger, this wrist I was showing and burning. Maybe these are small rebellions compared to the orgiastic cliché teens on TV, with their copies of *Playboy*, herbs for smoking, and mugs of Mom's vodka. These rebellions were what I could manage, though, and rebellion is limited to what you can see, where you know to go. If I went to the high school, by all those donuts, what would I become? How much more self-control could I lose before, well, I don't know. I never knew.

At night, I didn't sleep. The real demons were coming for me again, to kill me or fuck me—they seemed like the same thing at the time. I saw them, in that funny interval of vision, floating above my bed and pooling my blood in previously ignored areas. It was a possession from inside. My body was turning against me, was turning me on. I touched myself, and it meant something new, made things change, made me express myself unclearly. I didn't know, just yet, how to envision someone else's hands where mine were now. It was all a memory from before me, and I was wrong to have it. I knew that sex was powerful, caused people to risk their immortal souls. To have sex, to be in this body, was such a terrible crime against God as to be a death of kinds. No sleep for me, no dreams, trying to stay awake, to keep the sex away. My insomnia made me sleepy in class, unable to pay attention to the very person I'd impersonate later in the day. I wasn't doing my homework. Failed exams.

"What's wrong?" some adult amalgamation asks me, a mother, not a father, just a meddling deacon.

And I say, "I don't know."

And it's like they're trying to walk around me in words. "Why are you doing this?"

And I say, "I don't know."

A couple more steps, in words, to see me in 360, to finally spot the rot.

"What are we going to do about this?"

A blessed trinity completes. A mystery of faith: I am but I don't know.

I know it's wrong, to you, maybe you, I don't know you.

I say "you" so you know I'm thinking of you, hoping I can get you to come with me for a while, to where we're going. If I say "you" and you hear your name just once or twice—kismet, magic, and we never need to know why.

Some part of me was displacing another. Church ladies thought it might be a demon who interloped in my mind and body. The touches, fingers, and flames weren't mine but a hellish import against my better will. I waited for the demon to leave, prayed for its departure, for a sign I might be me again.

Another sign came, printed on thin Xerox paper. It told my mother and me to vacate our home within ten days or face things a child can't quite understand but knows to fear. I didn't want to leave the house. It was bright yellow, and I'd painted my bedroom sky blue. The backyard had two rosebushes and a pear tree. I was never patient enough to wait for the pears to ripen and instead made myself perfectly sick on sharp, hard fruits. Our next-door neighbor, Dagmar, was an older woman who'd emigrated from Slovakia. She taught me about the daylilies and mint that grew on the north side of the house, speaking patiently from her side of a border hedge and pointing across the property line. No one in my family had an accent, came from anywhere beyond these rivers. No one grew mint or daylilies. I had never even imagined what all those candy canes had hoped to simulate, never imagined daylilies might grow at my side. Each species spread by antipathetic underground structures, corms, maybe. Maybe stolons, or rhizomes. A conflict zone formed, a dead patch where each plant had strangled out the other. Season to season, the patch shifted as daylily or mint rallied.

In Dagmar's garden was a statue of the Virgin Mary, her holy head protected by a plastic cup that doubled as a measuring scoop for fertilizer. This devotion to God was unlike mine, with iconography verboten in my own Protestant sect. The sacred woman commanded precious space in Dagmar's garden but did not frighten her. I had nothing like this, just a floppy Bible I'd been given at Christmas. I worried that God would never forgive me if I got the cover wet or tore a page. The Bible had no sculptural heft, couldn't endure the elements, couldn't grow my garden with me.

A daydream: Mary Miracle-Gro lifts me over the short hedge that separates our houses, moves me into something like an embrace, or a hand holding mine, guiding me, and we're planting something new, or digging something up. Whenever the rains come, Dagmar puts cups on our heads.

When the eviction notice appeared, my mother was working at least two jobs. She did what she could to provide after her husband ditched, but she had limited education and work experience. He'd ditched because of sex and the sex he could have with a woman twenty-some years his junior. That woman hated me. I hated them both, and all that sex. Even with help from my older siblings, we couldn't keep up with the rent payments. The landlord let it go a couple times, but, finally, he became fed up. We packed up our things before the constable arrived. What was happening had come to feel inevitable, but, at the same time, church members told us to have faith: God wouldn't let us end up on the street. To an extent, they were right. We didn't end up on the street, but it was Pauline—and not God—who intervened.

Pauline lived in West Leechburg. Somewhat recently widowed, she was part of a cadre of churchwomen who made mysteries happen. In her case, she manifested the communion host—a rich pound cake cut into one-inch cubes. Bernice was Pauline's helper in ecclesiastical deeds. Pauline made dessert sacred, but Bernice made dessert social. Everybody grew zucchini in the summer, grew so much of it, even though nobody seemed to be sure what to do with it except shred it, sweeten it, and hand it off. Zucchini bread is gardening's abundance transposed. Bernice brought zucchini bread and more-loved confections to our "fellowship dinners"—informal potluck luncheons that followed Sunday services. She managed all the Crock-Pots and coffee percolators, got your soggy salad a respectable spot on the folding table full of dishes.

Sorry—I don't know if it's your salad, but I'm confident that you, a you out there, has made a soggy salad. Maybe you don't even know why. It's OK. Bernice has got a spot for you, for it.

Pauline had a spot for my mom and me after we were evicted. It was a trailer previously occupied by her son, who she described as a sort of hippie flop. He was somewhere else now. I don't remember where, and I'm not sure Pauline knew at the time.

How much was the rent? Couldn't tell you. Enough to matter. Enough to worry you if you were me.

A stand of tall hedges and trees gave the trailer's entrance privacy from the road. Along the front of the trailer Pauline had built small herb beds with "purple basil." The basil leaves had a concentrated taste of pepper and clove. I'm not sure it was basil at all. Herb names wander, change position relative to the plants they're supposed to identify. It's like how lilies have nothing to do with day or peace, and "grass" can mean a big patch of plants you've never looked at closely: sedges, clover, violets, daisies. Behind the trailer was a steep slope leading to abandoned garden beds and a couple fruit trees. The apples were too wormy to eat, and I still couldn't wait for the pears to ripen. The Sunday after we moved in, Pauline marched us over to Bernice's pew to tell her the good news.

"They're living in Jim's old trailer. I let them move in." Pauline wasn't much for telling stories.

Bernice nodded a distracted nod, her mind on Crock-Pots and squash gone rampant.

Back at the trailer, our garden beds had no zucchini, but other plants were out of control. The runs of "grass" that led up to the hedges and trees were in need of mowing. It was some day in spring or maybe fall, any time other than winter, when Pauline knocked on our front door.

"Here, use this mower. It will help you get strong."

Later that day, I would see Pauline's mandarin electric mower across the street, whizzing between prolific vegetable plots. Right now, though, she was shoving a rusty mechanical lawn mower at me. The handlebars roughed my hands and made them no good for holding food or flowers. I took the lawn mower from her and pretended—with such sincerity that only now do I know how much I was pretending—to be grateful. I admired Pauline's staunch attitude and fondness for hard work. Every morning, she beat the sun to the heat, warming her oven to bake the bread dough she'd mixed in the night. A loaf from the previous day rested partially eaten on the counter. She'd give it away or maybe feed it to ducks—I'm not sure. In the midday glow, she weeded her garden, gathered drinking water from a neighbor's spring, and returned calls from other church ladies. She mumbled a little Ukrainian to a neighbor who knew how to mumble back. Afternoons were for Bob Ross and following his instructions. The curved entryway walls of her home were a pastoral mural. Her home said it clearly: "I work here."

Giving the mower a good shove, I tried to get its cyclonic blades whizzing. It squeaked and grated on itself before giving a thump to a couple shoots of grass. The grass was too tall, and probably the blades too dull, for any satisfactory action. I lifted, repositioned the mower. I tried other angles, upslope and downslope. No. I was embarrassed.

Stuck.

Halting.

Breaking. Turning red with embarrassment. I wanted Pauline to know I was a hard worker, a good worker, just like her.

We're only living in this trailer because something happened, something odd. OK? The rent's late? I guess it's too high. I mean, sorry, I'm not tall enough. That's what I meant to say. The world is a little wonky like that. But God's on the case. Let's just all go inside, stay inside. Don't answer the door if it's Pauline or the police, grass or basil, telling us to get out, telling us to just push harder.

I couldn't tell Pauline the mower didn't work. That would have meant she had given me a lazy mower, and that was something she'd never do. She wasn't lazy. I parked the mower on the concrete slab patio at the trailer's front door and told myself I'd figure it out.

Before I figured it out, though, a fist was knocking against the jalousie window of our front door. It was Pauline again. A week or two had gone by, and the grass was still unmown. It looked "bad," and the neighbors were going to complain, she warned. Neighbors had complained about the lawn around the yellow house in East Vandergrift too. Someone lent us a lawn mower there too. That one was heavy, and you had to pull a cord to get it going. An abrupt drop in the lawn, indicating a lot gone empty, pulled the mower away from me, against me. I was certain I was about to lose a foot to the high-powered noise. I figured my older brother would take care of it. He didn't. The neighbors complained.

Now, my mother told Pauline I'd take care of it. I tried again with the rusty pusher—so *brute*. Sweat dripping, muscles aching, while dirt and bits of plant coated my shinbones and made me itchy. It was the kind of thing my brother did, my brother who spit out big brown globs of tobacco mucus, slept in late, and listened to music that sounded like unattractive cars crashing. Reticent and nonreligious, he was a worrying presence. I did not want to be like him, a man mowing grass. When Pauline mowed grass, it looked like getting what you want—clean lines of landscaping and the power of artifice. Mower-rust red and grass-stain green were the colors of men, but men didn't heat the Crock-Pots, place the salads, bake Christ's cake. I didn't want to mow the grass and didn't want to find a way to want such a thing.

Past the too-tall grass, an ordinary bus waited to take me to my new school. Our move had crossed district lines, into the Leechburg Area School District. Leechburg Middle was a sort of midpoint between the elementary school where I'd been and the high school I feared, but it was also an alien place. Everyone at Leechburg knew each other from the prior six years of education, but I knew no one.

At Leechburg, I studied Russian three days a week with a teacher who was late every day except Friday. In an accent my family feared, she'd ask, "Как вы сгодние?" "How are you today?"

In unison, the class would answer, "Очень хорошо, спасибо." "Very well, thanks."

She didn't teach us any other possible replies. We'd return the question to Marie (known in this class as Maria Ivanovna), but I can't repeat her answer. She didn't teach us those words either, whatever it was she mumbled to herself while rolling her eyes and shoving blond curls behind her ears. Across the hall was the algebra classroom. The algebra teacher was old friends with the Russian teacher, and between classes they would chat words still unknown in the hallway. On a Wednesday, after leaving Maria Ivanovna's class, I crossed the hall to the algebra classroom and took my seat. The algebra teacher handed me a freshly graded exam. He'd written "очень плохо" at the top. I recognized "очень"—"very." I asked, hopeful, what "плохо" meant.

"Bad," he said.

I'd lost my fight with the demons, gone hopeless. I tried to escape by falling asleep in class and becoming mysteriously ill with fevers, then going to the nurse's office for variable patches of time. It wasn't working, though. Each morning, my mother loaded me onto the bus beyond the hedges, and I headed back to the middle school. The precise timing of morning television commercials meant that the front door opened just as Connie Francis, being used to sell God only knows what, sang a slow-voweled question: "Who's sorry now?"

I could go slower than Connie, going down the narrow hall of the trailer. My bedroom was at the far end, away from the front door and kitchen. The front door was aluminum and weighted by the glass panes that would have let light in if curtains weren't kept stretched across them.

"I don't want people gawking in," my mother complained—as though anyone but a deer might walk by.

The door slammed with its own momentum as I left for school. In a preemptive answer, my hollow, wooden bedroom door slammed open each morning. I was midway between slammable doors one morning, season indeterminable, when my right leg buckled. Knee and ankle splayed, as my weight hit the overtrod carpet. The sniffles, the guts, the aching skull—I'd tried all the other put-on ailments to keep myself at home. So maybe it makes sense that my collapsed body did not signal real trouble to my mother. She kicked my stuck-out leg and watched my face. I don't know what face I made, but it was incongruous with her expectations.

The doctors explained that a bone in my spine, strained as much as the rest of me by "becoming a man," had fractured. A minor fracture, but it had caused other strains. Muscles? Discs? Who knows—not me. The pressure had, for just a few minutes, paralyzed my leg. So I fell. So I really couldn't go back to that school. Not for a while.

I'd tell you more, but it's a montage of doctors, hospitals, tests, begging for rides to appointments, prayer circles. It's bureaucracy and its intensification. It's too powerful, and if I go down that road, we'll never get back to that ugly school with the Queen Anne's lace.

That's where I wanted to end up anyway. From my thick, plastic back brace I bellowed to my mother to let me attend the Christian school. At the ugly little school, architectural austerity transformed pupils into humble comrades. The day's work began with sincere prayer for one another and a resonant knowledge that we were joined in a metaphysical struggle. Cooperative in our aspirations, encouraging in word and deed, sympathetic to our shared adolescent hurts. I took shallow breaths full of these dreams as I pleaded with my mother to send me there, pleaded with the pastor/principal to admit me even though we had no money for tuition. They each gave in to me, but each differently. I was permitted entry to those ugly doors if my mother would clean the building in the evenings. Now, all my demons would go silent, peer pressured by God's gleaming youths.

If you're reading this, I'm sure you already know that wasn't the case. The ugly school wasn't any better. God, being the most impotent man I can imagine, can't do anything about class inequity, poverty, or the body slashing we call sexual socialization. If he could do something, he wouldn't have come up with all that in the first place. He would've seen it all in the future and canceled the test run in the garden.

"It's going to be a shit show," he would've said to no one in particular.

All the kids at the Christian school knew each other from that school or from their churches, which were not my church. I was still the weird, curly-haired fag, "fag" being said a little more completely, if quietly.

"Hey, Tommy, stop that."

Teachers admonished Tommy for whispering "fag" as I walked by. The correction was about volume and not content. He wasn't wrong to call me that, but the teacher shouldn't be able to hear it. Better to ask me where my clothes came from or smile with a bitten tongue to say, "What kind of car does your mom drive?" when you know she drives nothing at all.

I helped my mother clean sometimes.

"Excuse me," squeaked from my throat as I reached around teachers' legs so I could get the trash cans under their desks. I saw bits of grades and unhappy notes, scraps of paper that acquired new complaints each time one teacher handed it off to the next.

"Bus duty. Kill me."

"Katie forgot her pills again."

"Can't afford to pay us, but there's a new fax machine?"

Other tasks were wordless. I was assigned to clean the boys' bathroom since I was a boy and my mother was not. Each heartbeat in that room was a pulse of a wish, for each and none of them to find me there. Dropping their flies, dropping out flesh as tense and flush as my own. I wanted us all to catch each other being naked, but not while I was scrubbing a toilet, not while it felt like I was cleaning the shit and piss from their bodies. Eyes hazy, pupils open like a mouth. Holding a toilet brush, young knees on old tile. Arm unmoving, and I hear footsteps. Paralytic. Please don't see me in here,

except to see me, undress me, find me breaking down under this back brace, and tell me I'm here now, and my back never broke, and I can push a lawn mower, can want to push a lawn mower, but I don't have to. You're coming with me, we're going together, into the thick marsh, into the Queen Anne's lace, lost in the weeds growing from our bodies.

Just a horny fag scrubbing the shitter. Good God, is this what you meant to make?

I left the Christian school after a year or so. Another back injury emerged from the first one. Then I returned to the school. My mother had started driving, and she would drop me off in the early morning, an hour or so before other students arrived. I wandered the plot of land around the ugly school. From the main driveway that connected church to school, a muddy track diverged and wandered perpendicular, away from the busy roadway. I followed it into Queen Anne's lace and cattails, then through woody nightshade and maple.

The grass is tall here, and the mower blades are broken, smashed up, formed into wind chimes. The wind doesn't know where this is. Sound doesn't stop at property lines or city limits.

My neighbor's saying hi again, offering the lawn mower again. I'm saying "no thanks" again.

I still don't want it, whatever it means to mow a lawn, and I don't mean to want it, either. My eyes refocus, and I see I'm in Swissvale, not East Vandergrift or West Leechburg or outside that school. My neighbor doesn't mean to cut me down, but there's only so much a lawn mower can do.

Holly

Leechburg, Pennsylvania (1999, maybe)

Fall down the hallway, and slide out the door where Pauline's knocking, and wait for a wood-paneled station wagon to drive us to church. That station wagon's always running late, and now I'm running, late.

My feet were clammy in my nylon dress socks by the time the station wagon arrived. I'd heard stories of why my mother didn't drive—insensitive instructors, crummy cars, fiddly roads. Without an independent means of transit, we relied on a faction of church ladies who drove us around. This week, it was Marina's turn to ferry us to Sunday services. The invariability and extremity of Marina's lateness were cartoonish, maybe mythological. She wasn't just late to everything but was late by one or two hours. Precisely when it seemed time to slip off all shoes and give up on the day, Marina's silly automobile would grumble up to the pickup point, buoyed by exhausted tires. Her long bob would percuss as she simultaneously tried to blame and castigate her three sons for making her late. Or had the plumbing been to blame? Or a long-winded telemarketer who'd met his match? (Marina's phone calls to my mother spanned three or four hours. My mother spent most of the call doodling silently in the margins of the white pages.) By the time Marina would arrive, all anticipation had cooled. Wherever she took you was simply a fact of travel now. Marina was at least an hour late that Sunday, but I remained antsy through the waiting.

I arrived late, running late, running toward my Sunday school classroom. A thin corridor of unfinished floorboards and sheets of drywall marked where our church's second floor transitioned from Sunday school classrooms into an apartment. Before God's people moved in, the building was a storefront, a shoe shop, maybe. For several years, the second floor had accommodated the first family. Now the pastor and his wife had their own house, and the church had reclaimed the upper rooms.

I rushed toward one of those upper rooms, seeking an answer to the moral and mortal crisis of my days: one of those ferrying women had been told to leave the congregation and never return.

Holly, the pastor and church elders asserted, was a witch.

What precisely it meant to be a witch in the lingering satanic panic of the 1990s is difficult to pin down. Maybe you identified with Dharma, not Greg, or you bought organic produce. The blending of New Age philosophy with the burgeoning health foods market meant crystals and organic broccoli might imply the same thing. In both cases, God's right to rule over life and health was being challenged by noncanonical means of healing or suspiciously earthy ways of eating. Ours was a God of industrial agriculture and the TV dinner. He was a man of the moment: Ore-Ida instant spuds and what's for dinner.

Evidence of the underworld arts could be found on a shopping receipt. Women in our church regularly railed against the Giant Eagle Advantage Card, a member's club card that entitles shoppers to the occasional discount on prunes or Ajax dish detergent. In the '90s I knew, the card was seen as an invasion of privacy and an instantiation of apocalyptic biblical prophecy. Revelation 13:17 tells of a day when no one shall be able to buy or sell goods without first receiving a marking from the Antichrist, the nemesis God literally created so He'd have a final plotline in the series *Earth*. It was a badge of unfrugal pride to shop without the card, to declare you'd rather lose cash than your soul. Never mind that you could buy whatever you wanted without an Advantage Card. The store would never punish you or deny you your pork chops for being cardless. That was beside the point. Inside the voluntary card lurked the possibility of a mandatory card, and only the vigilant would remain without blemish.

Holly wasn't a card-carrying witch but claimed another possession of power. Holly was a prophetess, chosen by God during a tent revival to speak on behalf of heaven. In her entryway closet, Holly kept the nondescript wooden folding chair she'd stolen from the convention center–turned-house of worship where she'd received her calling. The reverse side of the backrest was marked with bold letters, indicating the venue. On occasion, she'd pull the chair from the closet. A small group of us would marvel at the rickety seat, infinitely stronger than it appeared, and wonder if sitting in the chair might give us the same powers of foresight.

Who God had chosen as spokesperson: an eminently affable woman in her early forties, originally from upstate New York, with three kids, living in the demo double-wide of her mobile home community. She was a former burnout, having spent her youth floating through equally burnt-out industrial towns on a wave of booze, drugs, and hippie songs. She wore thick, full-coverage Pan Stik foundation by Max Factor on her full, white face. Her smile was slightly nervous, like she was hoping for happiness and sharing the vulnerability of hope in a bid of good faith. Her hair was a generic, longish bob, edges curled under, bangs feathered to the front. She laughed and sought in the church a holy reason to laugh—sought a replacement for the high of her New York years. Some way to feel good without the chaser of feeling bad. She was open about her own foolishness. Once, she drove over a sizable pothole that violently shook her entire minivan. She hit it at full speed, distracted by her children arguing in the third row. When the shaking stopped, she counted heads in the rearview mirror. All there. She began to laugh: "I thought the motor of the van had fallen out! I know that's not possible, but I really thought the motor had fallen out, right onto the road!" She chuckled at her gaffs and foibles. "Uh-doy!" she said to herself, in that way the slang of teenagers becomes the rote of moms.

Holly's prophetic ministry took form during errands in the Kiskiminetas Valley's three larger towns: Vandergrift, Leechburg, and Apollo—as well as their North/South/East/West/Heights/Extension subdivisions. Apollo, originally named Warren, is the oldest of the three and began as a salt-mining town. Leechburg was founded next, followed by Vandergrift—a planned and failed utopia, built by steel bosses to house anti-union mill workers from Apollo and attract a loyal workforce from elsewhere. The pre-European histories of this valley are not easy to come by. They were cleared away like the rocks blasted from hillsides to form roads along the river—something thought to be gone, though its absence (real or not) presents an instability. Something's always crumbling. Holly's van sped between what was and what was missing, through long-cleared stands of staghorn sumac trees and roadside cliffs hogtied with steel wire. Early in the area's settler history, the Valley was a literal backwater situated along the Kiskiminetas River, a tributary of the Allegheny River, which slices through Pittsburgh. The Kiski was too uneven in depth, too riddled with rapids to be used for commercial transportation. The surrounding terrain was no more compliant. Despite being relatively close to Pittsburgh, the Valley remained somewhat isolated until railroads came. I sensed this isolation. If it didn't exist in the Valley, it didn't matter—said of both threats and cures. Pittsburgh was where someone went, via helicopter, when they'd been injured so badly that local doctors couldn't be of use. Or it was the place someone went to be a fallen woman. It wasn't a big city to which we aspired but more a capital that demands cultural tribute. The three towns—Vandergrift, Leechburg, Apollo—were stops on a circular train, and if this came with a sense of self-sufficiency, it also came with a feeling of claustrophobia.

When I was four years old, my mother caught a ride from our home in Vandergrift to a children's prayer service in Leechburg.

At the front of the church hall, some Bible story was told, probably with puppets or Velcro-backed paper cutouts moved across a felt board. A grown-up asked the gathered, "Who wants to invite Jesus into their heart?"

I see my back, covered in a light blue shirt. I see my brown hair trimmed boyish and tidy. I'm shooting up to the front of the room. I'm saying a prayer, the only prayer I've ever said outside of a bedtime recitation. Something I've done has excited all the grown-ups, and everyone's happy. This is good, I feel, even if I don't know what it is.

It's not clear to me why we went that day. The timing couldn't have been worse—or better, depending on perspective. Not long after that first church visit, my father ditched. My newly single mother took refuge in the religious community, which consoled her, encouraged her, promised material support. They brought us in close, offering food and something more important: truth in a monopoly. In the eyes of pastor and congregant alike, our church wasn't *a church* among many. It was *the church*. People who attended other congregations elsewhere were misled at best, suspect of satanic intent at worst. We prayed that "unsaved" family and friends wouldn't just come to Jesus but would also come to us and sit alongside us in the chilly storefront-turned-sanctuary. Each day of the week had its own religious service, and these were joined together with men's meetings, women's gatherings, Bible studies, and telephone prayer phone trees. Powerfully, the church reoriented us relative to the world. Whatever bullying or torment my cool, secular peers might bring me at school, I knew it wasn't because I was *what they said I was*. It was because they were jealous, demonically envious of my personal relationship with God. I pitied them as much as I hated them as much as I desired to be them.

We stopped into church throughout the week, but Sunday took precedence. Each Sunday, congregants would line up to meet the pastor at the front of the church. There he would pray over them with hands extended. An invisible force would strike them, and they would collapse, seemingly unconscious, onto the floor. "Slain in the spirit" was the everyday term for this. Open-eyed women would adjust the skirts of their sisters in Christ, which had been lifted by the holy fall. Sturdy men would pull horizontal worshippers along the rough carpet to ensure there was always a clear spot for the next body. Some bodies would tremble. Other bodies would be so peaceful as to imply a sacred death.

Meanwhile, a tubby man with lacquered hair would boom out sounds in the lingo of heaven: "Ashunda ba ba ba rasabana. Ohhh, wa sa nakatakititikini." This was "speaking in tongues," the encrypted messages promised to followers of Christ in the New Testament. Minutes later, a bony widow would tremble to the front of the church and whisper to a deacon that God had given her the translation. She would take the microphone and, through gentle tears, tell us all what God had said when He said "Ashunda ba ba ba rasabana." It might be something about abortion or disobedient children. A loop was completed: from God, through his encoding device, into a speaker, into a decryption key, and into my ears. The message would send somebody—maybe me—flying to the floor next, body crumpled by the weight of God's words. I'd cry out my own quiet "Ashunda ba ba ba . . . rasabana."

Holly's minivan was both an extension and diversion from this church program; a mobile revival tent. Maybe it was the distribution of housewife errands that kept Holly in her van at all times, or maybe she was just one of those people who hates to sit at home. In shopping center parking lots, she would preach out her driver's side window to fellow church ladies. Or she'd linger at a stop sign on a quiet country road, just her and the other driver she'd flagged down. She spoke with the tone of someone who knows something about you that you wish she didn't.

"How's your husband?"

The other driver would sit quietly, uncomfortably, in their car and Holly's question. "He's doing fine."

An unconvinced "uh huh" would come from Holly. "Well, the Lord's been putting him on my heart."

The other driver might've asked herself quietly, "What does God know that I don't? What's He telling her?"

Whatever your secrets, there was always the possibility that God had told Holly, and she might tell someone else. God's gossip. Maybe your husband was addicted to pornography and there was no evidence and you'd never seen him with a "magazine," but God had told Holly and so it might be true, or at least true enough that you felt you had to answer for the accusations of sinfulness. Holly had no official position in the church, and the pastor did not seem to recognize her prophetic calling, but paranoia predominated the assembly. When a discount card can turn one evil, how many ways must there be to becoming the enemy? Who can be trusted? There were whispers about those who had become "backslidden"—a hideous compound word for someone who'd lost their footing on the path to holiness. It's a word reserved for those who've snuck a drink, a fuck, a foul-mouthed comedy. Backslidden was almost worse than being unsaved, worse than never finding our church in the first place, because you should know better than to let it happen to you. It's a sin of knowledge.

My mother and I found ourselves in Holly's van fairly often, at least as often as we were in Marina's station wagon. She drove us to church sometimes, to the grocery store or post office other times. Holly might ask my mom to come along on errands, someone to keep an eye on her kids while she popped into the store. Sometimes it was summer, or sometimes it was winter break. If I wasn't in school, I was in God's school, a white Dodge Caravan. When my spine gave up or gave out, Holly's van was where I convalesced. A bone cracked up, a disc slipped out. The pain was miserable, but it was also an escape from public school, where I took quick steps to bypass all eyes and lips, to get away before they could say what they were thinking and before I could think it myself. There were sympathetic girls, classmates, who still thought they might catch my eye. They worked in tandem with teachers who encouraged me to "man up." In my state, I was fragile and useless, and it was the job—of the doctor, the woman, the mill, the refiner's fire—to work me until I was toughened and ready to serve a purpose. And would I survive the reworking?

Wearing a back brace that resembled melted-down milk jugs, I sat in the middle row of Holly's van and accompanied her and my mother as they made their rounds. A broken body was a site of possible miracles, and there was hope in my infirmity, at least for the two women and their compatriots. It seemed every middle-aged woman in our church had her hands pressed against my cast, begging God for a miracle. There was shouting in English and weeping in tongues. Secretly, perhaps even to themselves, I think they wanted the miracle because it meant getting me back to school, where my more fundamental cracks might be repaired through socialization. When I was feeling generous, I'd claim that their prayers did something. "Less pain, more movement," "feeling hopeful for returning to school." Other days, I refused healing and reported back post-prayers, "No real change."

The message of Holly's van was a message of God's personal, direct, maybe scientifically demonstrable involvement in individual lives. Holly believed fervently that actual devils and angels waged war all around us, trying to gain an upper hand in a cosmic power struggle. She, and the other adults in my church, led me to believe the same. God would win these battles eventually, but he was a good sport and let his opponent get in a few shots. That's the whole story of Job, isn't it? God lets Satan up his score before telling him to lay off his kid. You can almost hear God's curtailing hail from Mount Something or Another: "Dude . . ."

Holly didn't just believe in these battling forces—she saw them. It's difficult to explain how this vision worked. On TV, psychotic hallucinations are overpowering breaks with reality. But Holly's visions weren't like that, and they weren't pathological in the same way. She knew with certainty that spectral entities were present but knew just as powerfully that others couldn't see them. That didn't make her feel crazy, though. It made her feel right. Her supernatural sight, a kind of analog augmented reality, was evidence that God had chosen her, had something to show her, something that perhaps others weren't ready to see. It was OK if they didn't see what she saw. The world wasn't out to get her, at least not any more than she was out to get the world.

When Holly saw an angel or demon it was, I surmise from how these visions were induced in me, like a double exposure: one image mapped across another, not quite sharing space and time but never fully removed from the same. Unlike the alien abductees of 1990s news television who reported feeling abandoned to ridicule and threatened by the ignorance of others, Holly took a stance of pity. The poor world—so much further from God's will than she was. They couldn't even see the angel in front of them. There, in the back of a Kmart, was a ten-foot celestial emissary, looking like something out of a hair metal band. He wasn't there the way the stock clerk was, but his image became part of how Holly interpreted the situation: God was there, with her. Maybe it was a show of solidarity or a sign of spiritual combat. Maybe the stock clerk was being divinely watched, kept safe through life's troubles by a force he couldn't see. Or perhaps his relaxed Kmart smock concealed his satanic ways (enacted behind dumpsters during fifteen-minute breaks in the parking lot, surely).

This sight was to become my own. As a young child, I would lay in bed at night and report to my mother that I saw "rainbows" and faces on the ceiling. Hypnogogic hallucinations, surely. The kind everyone has when they're tired and unable to live separate minds—a mind of reality, a mind of fantasy. My mother believed that God was showing me something. When we joined the church and came into Holly's orbit, my early rainbow sight was understood as proof that I'd been given the spiritual gift of "discernment."

Spiritual gifts, in my church's interpretation of the New Testament, were like magical powers doled out as godly inheritance to Christ's followers. Some had a gift of tongues, providing encrypted messages to the congregation. Others could interpret those messages and make them make sense on Earth. Some might be able to heal. I could "discern," could make distinctions between the spiritually pure and putrid. Routinely, I'd reveal, from the middle seat of Holly's van, some semihidden knowledge—such-and-such deacon was an adulterer or the occasional church visitor was a lesbian. I wasn't sure what a lesbian was, but someone older who was very certain about lesbians had implied the same, and I put it together with words. I peeled the name of the original speaker from the bit of knowledge. Now, I was the knower. Holly would coo, "Out of the mouths of babes." It was, to the adults, inconceivable that I'd listened in on all their signals. There was no possibility I'd surveilled them as God had, trying to keep myself steady amid the tumults of their behavior. No, what I knew had to be divine revelation—a sign that I, like Holly, had been chosen to know. It was also evidence that Holly, who had come to this unsavory sapphic information the old-fashioned way (gossip), wasn't wrong to condemn these sinning adults. God was heard to say not only "Dude . . ." but also "Girl . . ."

What metaphor could explain what it is to be told, as a young child, that you have been divinely selected to discern, to have a sort of existential taste? The descending canary or the nude emperor or the strip which sorts acid from base? A fool from the outset, a punchline? I wonder how this idea has inscribed itself into me, laid down a track. Am I, at times—which are almost always—quick to judge and determinedly opinionated, because I still believe that is my calling? Does the force of my feelings carry the mark of an old belief: that what I feel is somehow sovereign and eternal? Discernment became part of the narrative I told myself about myself, part of how I made sense of the world for my formative years. Always looking for the coincidence, adults in the church took my first name as additional evidence of my gifts: Daniel, Hebrew for, "God is my judge." I was told that I could see visions and so I *did* see visions. I had to see visions. How could my name be wrong?

I saw visions as Holly did, the same way you would if I asked you to imagine a cat on your lap or an apple on a tree. You will see what is describable, what does not break the conventions of physicality. We never saw creatures wholly beyond words, no colors outside the visible spectrum. Nothing erupted from underneath the material world, leaving it crumbled to the side. These were visions of language, logic, and human meaning. Descending a square stairwell in Leechburg Middle School, I would sense something was "off," and it wasn't me. Like Holly, I felt bad for a world that mistook me for something called "gay" when I was truly holy. What was wrong about this stairwell, what set my heart pounding, was not the vicious barb of my peers. It was a monstrous demon, shaped like a television dragon, resting at the base of the stairs. I saw it. I reported it to the adults in my life. They didn't see it as a valid reason to keep me home from school, though. But I knew I was in danger. A powerful force, something consumptive and callous was after me, planning to separate me from myself with its teeth, reform me in the gut. Every teen in the building was its messenger, and it was telling me to change or die.

The power of your visions correlates precisely to the power of your social standing. As a child, the things I saw might intrigue adults, but I had limited opportunity to take action on what I saw. Holly's visions led her to take drastic action, like refusing to pay rent to an "unchristian" landlord. Fervently, she told everyone in the congregation that God would supply for her needs. It was His will that would be done, and His will turned out to be theater.

He told Holly to form a prayer circle around her prefab double-wide. Women from the church, and a few women who'd fallen into Holly's orbit from elsewhere in the area, gathered hands to surround her house. They moved in a circular dance—something Holly was sure God ordained in the Bible, or maybe "Fiddler"? Some barked out chunks of word in a foreign, heavenly tongue. Others sang off-key. A few moaned and wailed. That was always the way to make sure people knew you were having a holy experience: moaning like you'd lost all self-control, all self-respect. You were just God's little loudspeaker, and heaven sounded like a very unconvincing porno.

"Oh God," Maryann would think to herself, knowing that she'd just taken the Lord's name in vain and would have to repent for that too. "I sound like Pam Anderson." Would she have dreamed along Pam's body, thinking of what newness she might have, or what familiarity she might jettison? Did she want, suddenly, irreversibly, to become Tommy Lee? Did she then switch to a quiet, whispered prayer? A declarative shout? Did she even know why she was there, or did she become lost in a vision of herself wearing out her Easy Spirits around a trailer on a rural road?

It's been so long now that I don't quite recall if God was supposed to be putting up a spiritual wall to keep the landlord out or tearing down a wall to independence à la Jericho in the Bible. There was a lot of spiritual wall building and tearing down in our church, maybe a ritual reenactment. No one had nuked anyone else in the Cold War, and both God and Satan seemed equally hesitant to fire the first shot. The energy swelled and fizzled. The trailer-side gentile hora would get super serious and warlike, then someone would trip on a shoelace. The stumble would make some people laugh, some people scowl.

"If you were holy enough, you wouldn't need shoelaces, Debra. God would hold your shoes on your feet. It says it clear as day in Ezekiel."

Amid this big game of Hokey Pokey, someone played shofar recordings on a tape player. Loose borrowing from Judaism was very chic among '90s Evangelicals. Someone else stomped their feet, maybe to shake hell. They prayed for Holly and against her landlord. The landlord—what would become of him if God should hear their prayers? That was never made clear. Would God forcibly convert him? Remove his legal ownership? Kill him?

None of these, it turned out. A week or so later, the constable came to evict Holly from her home. Was God unimpressed by the display? Did he forget to watch at all? It didn't have to be like this. She had the money to pay rent. Her husband worked in upstate New York, where they owned a house. He'd been trying to get Holly to move back up there, but God told her to stay in Pennsylvania. Now, she was—by some definition—homeless with three kids and two grandkids in her care, all because God told her to stop paying her rent. All six of them moved into a small mobile home along a dirt road abutting a creek. It was a mess, trying to get the kids to their schools, trying to get the van up the driveway in the winter. I don't know what God was thinking.

For some in our church, Holly's eviction was the final proof that her messages weren't actually from God at all. When I mentioned Holly to other adults in the church, they would sometimes reply with a cold politeness. They weren't going to tell a child that Holly was a fraud, but they also weren't going to disguise their distaste too thoroughly. I was already headed in the wrong direction, and they didn't want silence to form a signpost. Having a prophecy was one thing. Everyone had a prophecy at some point in their lives. Everyone had wailed and moaned during a Sunday service and then called out something or another about God being pleased or displeased with America and all the things that would come to "her" as a result. But being "a prophet," having that biblical calling? That was going too far. And a woman prophet? This verged on blasphemy.

Women were discouraged from teaching, literally barred from teaching men. "The husband shall be over all the house" or "is it right for man to listen to the wife?" or something in the Bible. I can't remember anymore. It was agreed, though, that a woman explaining God's message was suspect, and explaining to a man was mutinous. She was taking on too much power, and she'd never be able to resist its allure. Though Christians have almost forgotten the apocryphal myth of Lilith, it is resonant in their fears. Lilith was Adam's first wife, created from the dirt herself and sharing no rib with her husband. Lilith refused to be under Adam—literally or figuratively. Instead, she intoned the secret name of God, sprouted wings, and flew off. "Fuck you and the creation you rode in on." The myth goes on to say Lilith was cursed by God, as if that would be necessary. Isn't it a curse to live your visions? Isn't it a curse to be made an example of? The one who went mad, the one who refused to play ball, the one who didn't listen? Lilith's curse is every well-behaved person who ever lived, every cooperative team member. God's impotence in maledictive form is not required here.

Our church was always afraid that a woman would figure out how to take the reins, and, in that moment, she would glimpse something beyond the finitude of the church and Christ. She'd glimpse a sovereignty all her own. A woman who claimed to hear from God directly, to speak more clearly of his plans than men, that woman was already too close to this revelation. It wasn't only men who feared this leap but women too. The hazard of seeing someone jump is that it reveals to you that you, too, might jump, might wish to jump. Calling herself a prophetess became evidence that Holly *couldn't* be a prophetess. A woman could only be a prophetess by accident, humbly, innocently, in a sort of "dumb blonde" way. She'd never know it, bless her.

With grudging permission from church leadership, Holly hosted a women's Bible study on Tuesday mornings. Each week, a corps of middle-aged women made their way to the "fellowship hall" of our church. The hall had previously served as a sanctuary—the second of three in succession, as the church bought additional storefronts on the east side of its first building. Creaky floorboards painted a dark, glossy brown were scuffed by stacking chairs arranged around a folding table. Embroidered Bible covers flopped open, scattering cross-stitched bookmarks made on plastic mesh. They carried messages like "Peace" or "God Is Alive" and were decorated with chunky acrylic yarn crosses and embroidery floss blobs of white dove. Christ is kitsch, is a sort of anyone-can-buy-it product. A policy saying that everyone can be fashionable in heaven with minimal effort.

Holly's Bible study mimicked the workings of her television mentor, Joyce Meyer. In sports arenas around the country, the multimillion Meyer preaches a message of overdue prosperity and self-forgiveness, punctuated with dry, down-home wit. She's from Missouri, and through her drawn diphthongs she intones the agreed-upon television code of middle-class motherness.

Her husband? Smiling eye roll.

Her kids? Smiling eye roll.

"God, I'm glad you gave me so many gifts, but I might need the receipts to return a few."

We all laugh. It's hard being a woman, but that's being a woman, and the writers don't have any other ideas this season. Holly did her best to replicate Meyer's charming delivery. Some regular attendees of her Tuesday study were sure they were watching the next Joyce take shape, getting in at the ground level of God's next big thing.

But Joyce was always restrained. She spoke in tongues on television, but not too much. She laid off the miracles, and her acolytes didn't routinely fall out in spiritual seizures à la Benny Hinn. Hinn is a contemporary of Meyer's—a Palestinian American man in a Nehru jacket who seemed to fling his followers all around the convention center stage. "Be healed!" he'd shout with his hands moving forward, and then Granny would fly out of her wheelchair, crying. She was definitely being healed. Many people found Hinn a touch distasteful, and surely God caught onto this sentiment. Maybe God told Meyer not to scare the twenty-five- to thirty-year-olds in the Northeast market.

"It's an important market share," he told her during her morning prayers.

And Joyce didn't really prophesy, except for the prophesying required of all televangelists: "God is telling me that if you give $20 today, then you'll receive . . ." Holly couldn't afford not to prophesy, and her prophecies were daring. She predicted doom for the church if it purchased its third storefront. There was a curse of some variety on the land—satanic or Indian—and it was going to do terrible things to us: devil-possessed children, whoring wives, men becoming women. I don't think that last one was on anyone else's mind, but I'd picked up on the fact that such a transformation counted as a demonstration of God's fury. For church leadership, purchasing the storefront meant a better appearance for the church and more room for congregants to gather and give tithes. It also represented the success of our young, new pastor who'd taken over from his older mentor just a year or two before. Slightly older than the new cleric, Holly took a mothering tone with him. And why shouldn't she? She was chosen by God. He was chosen by a hiring committee.

I couldn't help but side with Holly. In her van, my catty tongue and overwrought facial expressions were part of a precocious charm. I sat quietly, didn't complain, didn't fight or beg for a stop at McDonald's. Instead, I took part in the ongoing religious project of sussing out the devils and angels of our riverside villages. The leaders of this project were women: the abandoned, the divorced, the "golf widows," and men weren't among their numbers so, by logical extension, I *couldn't be* a man. I was male. I was a boy. But I was not part (yet) of the troubled and troubling classification of "man." This temporary elision assuaged my pubescent worries. There was no time to become a man. These women and I were busy with not only ethereal tasks but also quotidian priorities: get milk, drop off check for Vacation Bible Study, see about getting a refund on that sweater. The to-do list was my puberty blocker.

In stark contrast, the pastor and his cronies represented the resurrection of my not-dead father. Having left my mother and I only shortly after we joined the church, my father was alive, if absent. I resented his absence and the space it opened. A parade of paternal apparitions, meant to make my father reappear in a new form, came toward me at church. There were invitations to camping or fishing trips, mandatory involvement in an Evangelical version of Boy Scouts, and forced sex-segregated recreational activities. I seemed to have nothing in common with these men. They did not seem to enjoy me much, but their fears of what I could become if they failed to father me outweighed idiosyncratic preference. Their fears weren't wrong. I was headed toward their very worst imagining of destruction, ruin, perversion, and satanic abandon. No one dared say anything about it, but my eyes lingered too long on the older teen boys with dark hair. Toward girls, I showed an unwelcome familiarity that implied that women might be friends, not targets. Much as I would relish wounding those old men by saying they put me on the path to Babylon, I know I was already en route. They only slowed me, gave me a funny story to tell the other whores upon arrival into that great city of waste. At the time, though, they made me want to evaporate and move unseen out the French doors from the sanctuary to the curb. I didn't want to leave my body; I wanted to leave their bodies, to become a fluid temporarily ungraspable, then terribly graspable. I wanted to defy the old men and submit to their sons. The men of the church had no appeal, not socially. Nothing was at risk for them in the way Holly risked everything by expressing (God's) opinion. The men already had the power, had the archival authority of God. They were emptied of life and full of certainty.

Holly was told to stop teaching. Complaints filtered together, lost authorial detail as they reached the pastor and he—more or less—conveyed them with his agreement. Holly had contradicted the elders of the church, questioned the leadership of the pastor. The women in Holly's orbit called our church "dead," told anyone who'd listen that God wasn't there anymore, had left any one of the buildings the congregation had bought. The leadership had disappointed him. The women began attending services in nearby towns where they'd heard of revival. They'd taken up wings, seeking their own revelations. The pastor rebuked her, them.

If this stung, it didn't stick. Holly kept prophesying from her van, kept asking people what they thought of the pastor's own spiritual qualifications.

"I mean, do you feel . . . I feel the Lord saying, '. . .'" Fits of stop/start became the syntax of sending out these questions. "I feel God's heart is *grieved*. Pastor Ron isn't listening to what He's telling him, and there will come a time. . . ."

Holly's face soured, her shoulders mounted toward her ears as a shiver sent her bobbed hair in a track around her face.

"Ewwww . . . I can feel it."

A vociferous condemnation of the pastor in the voice of God would only compound Holly's problems. She must've known that. So, instead, God was *hurt*, aggrieved by the insolent young leader, and now acidic recompense was coming this way. The body of a mother quaked and rolled, tears streaming down white skin. Is this Ruby Ridge? Waco? Who has inflamed the tender heart of the American woman, the woman who stitches the first flag, buries the dead soldier boy, births the middle class, rivets back together the wounded bells of liberty? This was the edge of an apocalypse more damning than the author of Revelations could have known, because this was a woman's apocalypse: full of fires kept in the walls, all the screams never given air to shake. This was the return of everything locked away in the asylum, and I was not mistaken: this kind of apocalypse would become my own freedom as too much bad feeling made walls of men into submerged gravel. I was desperate for God to push the button, launch the rockets, blow it all sky high. I needed God to kill the landlord, the pastor, the father, and leave me only with the mothers and their sons.

Those body-racking shivers were never backed by the blast of destruction I needed. Maybe all these quaking, mournful moments were small release valves that made it possible for everyone else to carry on society all the same. Holly vented to friends, and they all agreed the church was wrong, but the agreement defused them.

God was aggrieved, but the church was angry. One Saturday morning, the pastor and elders called Holly into the church offices, where they finally executed the power they'd to date only contemplated: they told Holly to leave the church and never return. She had been serving as church secretary, and so she was fired, too, but how could that matter in comparison to the house of God declaring her persona non grata? There was no recourse for her. Whatever command God had given her, it did not extend into this flipped storefront on the shores of the Kiskiminetas. She left the church, and her group of inspired women slowly eroded. Some women needed to stay in the church for support or social reasons, and there's that old verse about how you can't serve two masters. Others wanted to keep following Holly, but the wind had been knocked out of her. She became quieter, lonelier. She moved to New York finally.

Rushing from Marina's station wagon, I found my way into the Sunday school classroom where I'd found tutelage under Holly for several months. Pastor Ron sat in Holly's chair. He'd reclaimed what was his: the congregation, the future. My mother and I left the building before Sunday worship services began. Eyes followed us, the emissaries of a witch, as we moved through the conjoined storefronts and out the door. I knew the asteroids were coming, the godless internet cyborgs who would rip the congregants limb from limb. They'd rejected God's messenger, and now he wouldn't wait for Y2K to reveal the full biotechno hell he'd created for his own children. I thought they'd called down, from heaven and upon their heads, maximum disorder, misery, and insanity. This, too, was a vision.

Other Names

Leechburg, Pennsylvania (any time you like)

Step out the front doors of that church, and you'll be on Leechburg's main drag. Down the way from that church, just past the parking lot where Holly's van awaits, is the Leechburg Area Museum and Historical Society. I would take you to the museum in my memory, but what I've got in that archive is dust of uncertain provenance. I remember an old sewing machine, though that could have been my grandmother's in her house up the hill. I remember stiff, printed cotton curtains. Anyone's, really. I think the place has two floors, and you can take the stairs. All generalities.

Some things are remembered and some are forgotten, and it's what's in between that has the power. A thin memory is a sort of vision too. A flicker of something: misreading a billboard, knowing a scent is familiar but not why, calling someone by the wrong name, a name you've never said before or so you think.

Leechburg had other names. In 1850, mill owner David Leech humbly renamed the town after himself—Leechburg. He'd bought up all the acreage of the small settlement then known as "Friendship," so why not? The newly declared town had lumber mills, and eventually, the other sorts of mills came too. This era of Leechburg is characterized by the stuff you'd hear from a man with a gray beard full of party cracker crumbs: old churches, white ethnic strife, the flood of 1889.

What is less known, maybe less knowable, is what happened before all these names started stumbling along the riverside.

In a book he edited for Leechburg's 150th anniversary, Joseph Kantor imagines the area before European settlement as "pristine," with "sunlight glittering on the Kiski [River], lush forest overhanging the swift current. Game was likely plentiful and the flooding of the river made the soil rich." He admits, however, that this is all fantasy. Until the late 1700s, few European settlers lived in the area. Even in 1822, only eight white families could be found. What happened before those eight families, before settlers filed land patents with offices on the other side of the state, is treated by Kantor and others as open. Empty.

History's never been my thing. Not because I'm not interested but because I'm not satisfied. I put together all the pieces, the who's and what's and *I'm sure you went to elementary school*—but then I find I don't know what I mean to find. Like when I learned about Alois Auer.

Alois Auer was an Austrian printer who ran the Austrian state printing house in the mid-nineteenth century. Men like that always had money and time for hobbies, and Auer's hobby was botany. Like so many botanists, Auer wanted to make records from plants—the who's and what's and *you went to elementary school*'s of each species. Botanists were mostly unimpressed by early photography, and you can only coat a leaf in ink and press it to paper so many times before it disintegrates. Auer devised something he called *Naturselbstdrucke*—nature self-printing. In *Naturselbstdrucke*, a dried plant is pressed into soft lead, and the lead is then electroplated with a harder metal, like copper. The resulting plate can be used over and over. The system never caught on, for lots of reasons. I thought I was curious about the history of plant images, but when I came across Auer's story, I lost interest in my original question. Auer's story was the thing I was looking for, even if I don't know what it is. I still don't know why I was looking for Auer's story, but I stopped researching the history of plant images when I found it.

We want to imagine it, don't we? We, who look like the king's faithfully traitorous subjects, want to imagine the pristine glittering lush overhanging swift plentiful rich. We keep borrowing this desire from the past. We borrow it from the men who arrived on ships, looked around, and said "It's empty" into the eyes of living people. We borrow it, all hot and sweaty and dying to dig in before someone catches us. It's so empty, this desire. It's where the real emptiness is.

By all accounts, no Native groups took up the site of Leechburg as a permanent dwelling. The site wasn't far from a Native town (of unknown affiliation) but still a good distance away on foot. Native peoples of the Delaware River and Bay regions came through the area when they were displaced by European settlers from lands farther east. It's unclear, though, if they made any kind of settlement in the spot where Leech would make a burg. It seems like a place we, the we who can't see anyone as far as the eye can see, need to fill with history.

I could make the case that Native people were using the land even if they didn't live on it. Foraging grounds, fishing shores, and hunting woods all come to mind. But what about my yard, the one I hate to mow? If I don't mow it, if I don't use it for anything, is it still part of my home? If it's overgrown and I don't forage, don't plant, don't even look at it except to hate the lawn mower—is it possibly yours to build on and not mine to keep in abeyance? Who doesn't keep something useless at times, something they don't quite want? Nobody needed to work the land for the land to be working on someone.

The land was empty, if hunger becomes a source of fear. If more is taken than wanted. Eating yourself to sleep. All desires dulled. All senses crushed. All land indistinct. The eyes are filled with every seen thing, and no sensation of lack can enter. Every tract becomes empty in this way.

Empty like the address bar of a web browser, waiting for its cue. I type in "Leechburg history" and click "Go" because what I know about Leechburg is spectral. It's terribly real, that Leechburg full of things Holly saw, things I feared would eat me up. But I know now that I saw a Leechburg most residents did not—filled with cruel spirits whose names were revealed by sorcery. A woman of the church would flip the pages of her Bible and, at random, put her finger down on a shifting page, freeze the word beneath her prints.

"Leviathan."

The evil spirit she'd sensed—it was a Leviathan, living in the river just blocks from the church. Its name had been revealed through bibliomancy. I know now that people in the town museum, the district court office, the Mad Hatter bar, didn't live in a town with a satanic Nessie. So I type and click to figure out what, maybe, they did live with. The town museum website tells me about something I never knew, and I wonder how I never knew it. A factoid and an absence: two mysteries, two instances where the Leechburg I know doesn't appear. There's an empty lot where the church was, in my mind.

More typing and clicking leads me to learn that John Walker had the area surveyed in 1773. The following year, he sold a portion of the land to Joshua Elder. Nearly ten years later, Elder passed that portion on to Delaware Indian Chief White Mattock for five pounds, ten shillings. It's possible White Mattock wasn't an official chief, according to Kantor. White Mattock doesn't appear in *Indian Chiefs of PA*, a 1971 directory-out-of-time listing many of the Native leaders who had significant dealings with European, colonial, or American government forces. Histories of the town make special mention of White Mattock because he purchased the town "after the manner of the white man." His name is an outlier among the names of those who held that spot in the only manner they ever knew—William P. Brady, Jacob Mechling, Frederick Steif, Joseph Hunter, Matthew Shields, and (of course) David Leech. Following White Mattock's purchase, the area became known as "White Plains."

White Mattock probably never referred to himself as Delaware. "Delaware" comes from an honorific title given to colonial Virginia governor Sir Thomas West, also known as Lord de la Warr III. According to Brice Obermeyer, when Captain Samuel Argall explored present-day Delaware, he passed the name along in honor of West. The peoples of the bays and rivers nearby were Unami- and Munsee-speaking

Lenape peoples and had no reason to call themselves "de la Warr." Encroachment by and violence from Europeans forced many Lenape—called "Delaware" by white settlers—toward the western frontier, the area of Fort Pitt and Ohio. Some headed north, into New York and Ontario. The Lenape in Leechburg's Kiskiminetas River valley would have likely become "protectorates" of the Haudenosaunee (Iroquois) who claimed the land in the late 1700s. If Delaware Chief White Mattock was present in the area at the time, he may not have been welcomed as a neighbor in this New America. Obermeyer says that, although Lenape people living in the Pittsburgh area largely sided with American colonists in the Revolutionary War, they were still seen as "defeated British allies" in the end.

We know of Delaware Chief White Mattock's land purchase because of a man named William Riley Trout. A lifelong resident of the Leechburg area, William Trout was born in September 1829 and became known locally among whites as an expert in Native history. He was a teacher, a Mason, a father, a husband—all the things a descendant of German immigrants might become. Trout doesn't appear to have published on Native history in his lifetime, but his knowledge was passed along by people like T. J. Henry—a physician in the neighboring town of Apollo. In 1916, Henry published a tome celebrating Apollo's first century. Under the heading "LEGENDARY," Henry writes that "the late Wm. Trout, a local historian of note, was of the opinion . . . that White Mattock, Warren and Shelocta were all Indians who had taken out patents for land after the manner of the white man. White Mattock had taken up the site of Leechburg."

According to Henry, Trout's information on White Mattock is confirmed by another text, Robert Walter Smith's *History of Armstrong County, Pennsylvania*, from 1883. It's a chain of custody. Trout told Henry there was a Delaware chief named White Mattock who owned the land that became Leechburg, and Henry says Smith's book confirms Trout's story. You won't find White Mattock, Delaware chief, in Smith's *History of*

Armstrong County, though. Henry's citation, Trout's confirmation, isn't on those pages. In White Mattock's place is another man: White Matlock (lock like a door, not tock like a clock). Smith tells us White Matlock obtained the same 192.5 acres from Joshua Elder that White Mattock supposedly obtained. Smith doesn't mention Matlock's chiefly status or his other-than-Euro designation.

Smith's omission is a tunnel, leading back nearly one hundred years. In the late 1700s, a group of European Americans in New York formed a local chapter of a social organization for hyperpatriotic, very American Americans. With no irony in their little colonial hearts, they named their organization after a Native American leader—Tamanend. Tamanend, part of the Lenape people himself, was also known to white settlers as "Tammany." From this derivative, these early American flag fanatics drew their society's name: the Sons of King Tammany, then later the Sons of St. Tammany.

The selection of a Native American mascot like Tamanend wasn't random. Historian Philip J. Deloria has chronicled European Americans' repetitive practice of costuming themselves—literally or otherwise—in a cartoonish version of Native people as part of some political action or another. During the Whiskey Rebellion (1791–1794), a group of white antitaxation rebels penned a pseudodeclaration that mimicked the style of "Indian treaties." The treaty was published in the *Pittsburg Gazette* as a message from the "Six United Nations of White Indians." From behind semi-Native-sounding pen names, a group of tribal "Captains" lodged their protest. Wasn't this *their* rightful land, given to them by a white God? Who could impose taxes, tariffs, or regulations on God's gifts? In their message from the "Six United Nations," the settlers claimed an inalienable right to land, carried in their blood, borne into them by the very soil. They wanted to grow and distill unimpeded.

Tamanend, and Native people more generally, emblematized the "wild" spirit that white settlers hoped would keep them free and keep government interference in check. White settlers wanted an icon who was unbridled at heart, a potential menace to "the powers that be," made from corpuscles of unalienable aboriginal sovereignty. The Sons of St. Tammany made themselves a father in this image of a rightful rebel. Tamanend, the man, may or may not have seen himself as any of those things. (What we see in people is often what we need to see in them, and we've all had to live inside someone else's fantasy at times.) As the Tammanies grew, the Lenape people themselves were pushed farther west and north by people who sought to copy them to death. These copyists would dress in "native" garb, smear their faces with paint, and pass a ritual pipe as a sign of brotherliness.

A New York City directory from 1798 lists the who's who of the local Tammany chapter. Each person listed was styled as a "sachem"—the term for a traditional Lenape leader. Among them was a man named White Matlack. Born in 1745, in Haddonfield, New Jersey, White Matlack was a watchmaker, silversmith, brewer, and steel manufacturer. He opposed slavery and was expelled from the Quakers for supporting the Revolutionary War. His brother, Timothy Matlack, was the scribe for the Declaration of Independence. In 1783, White Matlack bought the same 192.5 acres of land along the Kiskiminetas River that Smith, Henry, and Trout erringly assigned to Chief/non-Chief Mattock/Matlock.

But why did Matlack make this purchase? There was certainly land speculation going on along the "Western frontier" at the time. Maybe he even entertained the idea of heading west himself. We know that Timothy passed through western Pennsylvania in the 1790s as part of a state-sponsored expedition. Whatever his reasons, *Pennsylvania Land Record Patent Books* volume AA15, AA16 shows that one White Matlack of Philadelphia—and not one White Matlock of places unknown, or one White Mattock of the Lenape peoples—purchased from Joshua Elder the land that would become Leechburg. Eleven years later, the same White Matlack would sell the land to Abraham Shoemaker.

Though there's plenty of evidence of Matlack's political and business endeavors in the eastern part of Pennsylvania, there's nothing to demonstrate he ever set foot west of the Allegheny Mountains. There's no suggestion I can find that he walked along the Kiskiminetas or ever saw the land named "White Plains." There were records of his purchase, though, and haven't you ever wondered about a great-grandmother you never met or the person who lived in your house a hundred years ago? There are records that they existed: your body now, the house now, and all that time before now. "Now" tells us something happened before, but the details get fuzzy. So we imagine and fabricate. We make the ghosts whose company we want to keep. William Trout collected ghosts, and T. J. Henry pressed them into book pages.

Have you ever seen a herbarium sample? Some very nice paper is laid out and a dried plant, carefully pressed flat when collected by a keen botanist in the field, is secured to the paper with little adhesive tabs. A minimum of tabs is used to keep the plant stable without obscuring the parts where stem meets leaf, or stamen flips from corolla. Botanists often survey where parts of plants join up or dissociate in order to identify a species or think about its ecological functions. Other things are attached to the paper, like labels showing who did the collecting, the pressing, the mounting. A museum might affix its stamp of ownership. It's not the full memory of a place or plant life, though. No buzzing dragonflies, no sodden smells. The herbarium sample is a specific answer to a specific question, a specific extract of time.

Trout and Henry were undoubtedly curious about names that floated around the Leechburg area, names that had very little context attached to them. White Matlack would have been among them, a landowner characterized by distances physical and temporal. They had to ask, "Who else was he? What else can this town mean?"

Hot, salty slices of pizza sizzling in a restaurant across the street from my church—a counterpoint to Christian asceticism;

a harmony to American gluttony. Next to the pizzeria, in yet another parking lot, the Red Cross drew a sample of my blood and graded it. B+, like my mother. Through the parking lot and across the railroad tracks, somewhere, and I was never very clear where, a house where my family lived long before I was born. But before that, an active mill downriver manufactured jobs. Before that, something lush. Someone pristine, unbothered by history. These are all dreams of Leechburg, isolated by the power of the want that animates them.

Getting what you want has a way of not lasting. Less than a century after the United States declared its independence, settlers began to worry that the *true* American way of life was being forgotten. The ideological virility of America was softening, and only a firm look back could bring things back around. Focused on patriotism, history, and charitable causes, the Improved Order of Red Men "painted itself as a gathering of historians, the worthy keepers of the nation's aboriginal roots," according to Deloria. Like the Tammanies, they dressed in costume. Unlike the Tammanies, they didn't think of Native people as a symbol of political power but as touchstones for a good, old, natural, All-American, meat-eating, firework-firing past that never was. Local chapters of the Order took on "tribal names," and used a faux-Indigenous jargon. A week was called "seven suns," and a year, "a grand sun." Taking a cue from social science fields like ethnography, the Improved Order of Red Men focused on Native people as treasures to be collected, though what they collected was largely their own fantasies about those people. In addition to mythologizing Native peoples, the Order was interested in reviving the legacy of early Tammany members, like White Matlack.

At least two chapters of the Improved Order of Red Men existed in the Kiskiminetas Valley: the Caughnewago tribe, no. 228, was established in Apollo in 1875; and the Accotonk tribe, no. 480, was established in Vandergrift in 1906. Somewhere in this time frame, William Trout told T. J. Henry the tale of Chief White Mattock, Delaware real estate innovator.

If Trout, the touted expert on Natives, joined one of those "improved tribes," it might explain why he told Henry that Matlack-turned-Mattock was a "sachem." Matlack was a Tammany, the kind of man that many whites of Trout's generation idolized: a skilled craftsman, a rebel against the crown, a patriot to his ruin. Trout would have wanted to celebrate Matlack's story. Perhaps Trout told T. J. Henry and others that Matlack was a sachem but forgot to clarify what kind of sachem he was. Henry got confused, published the confusion, and made authenticity from artifice.

Or perhaps Trout didn't even know about Quaker White Matlack, instead finding inspiration in fantasy. Fantasy looks for opportunity, a little handhold from which it can spread out. In the case of Matlack turned Mattock, the handhold may have been handwriting. In the margins of the *Land Record Patent Book,* the scribe noted the buyer for each transaction. Next to the entry for the Leechburg land, the scribe wrote "Patent to W. Matlack" in that heavily slanted, thin-lined 1700s script we know from Declarations of things. In a bit of flourish, the scribe crossed not only his t's but his l's too. The "a" was left ambiguous. (Ah-oh. A false start.) To a quick eye, "Matlack" looks like "Matlock," maybe even "Mattock." Trout could have misread the property book's listing for "White Matlack" as "White Mattock"—"White Mattock," like "Crazy Horse." Stereotypes about Native names did the rest. Just describing things, all sparkling, lush, rich. Then again, Trout thought that two other towns in the area were named for "Indian chiefs." Those tales seem to be no more true than the thin legend of White Mattock. White Mattock, Delaware chief, is a psychological specter. He's the dragon in my middle school, the Kmart angel, the river leviathan. Trout saw several things that weren't there, a little like Holly and I.

Questions with unknowable answers are a means to keep me busy. I look for somewhere empty to put my questions, bend and pose them like toys, cast them in the dramas that animate me. I make up an answer to my question. I answer myself. Empty out the question. Case closed. History written. Nothing to see. Like when you turn out the lights at night, get ready to dream, and the whole room seems so dark. But then your eyes adjust and closet door, dresser edge, lampshade all reassemble from gray static. Then, rainbows. The question—Who is Leechburg to me?—seems to go away, but I lose faith in the darkness into which I've submerged it. I see the question again. It's still there.

Used to be, we who look like White Matlack could imagine a White Mattock to tell us who we are, how we got to this place. It's wrong, we now say. And we know it doesn't work. We've become aware that what we're seeing is the Quaker Oats man wearing gemstone turkey feathers from JOANN Fabrics. We see the clipped coupons, the strip mall, and a couple sewing projects-to-be-abandoned. We're unsatisfied with the authenticity we've assembled from parts of elsewhere. We're looking for quiet from before a question, but we're made from the question. It's a futile maneuver. We're trying to see before we were conceived, just two gametes in two irreconcilable bodies. States forever un-united.

* * *

White Mattock was never there, but plenty of other people were: the Haudenosaunee, Lenape, Osage, and Shawnee. Give the town maps a rest and consider some other sources, like *Delaware Tribe in a Cherokee Nation*, by Brice Obermeyer, or *Playing Indian*, by Philip Deloria.

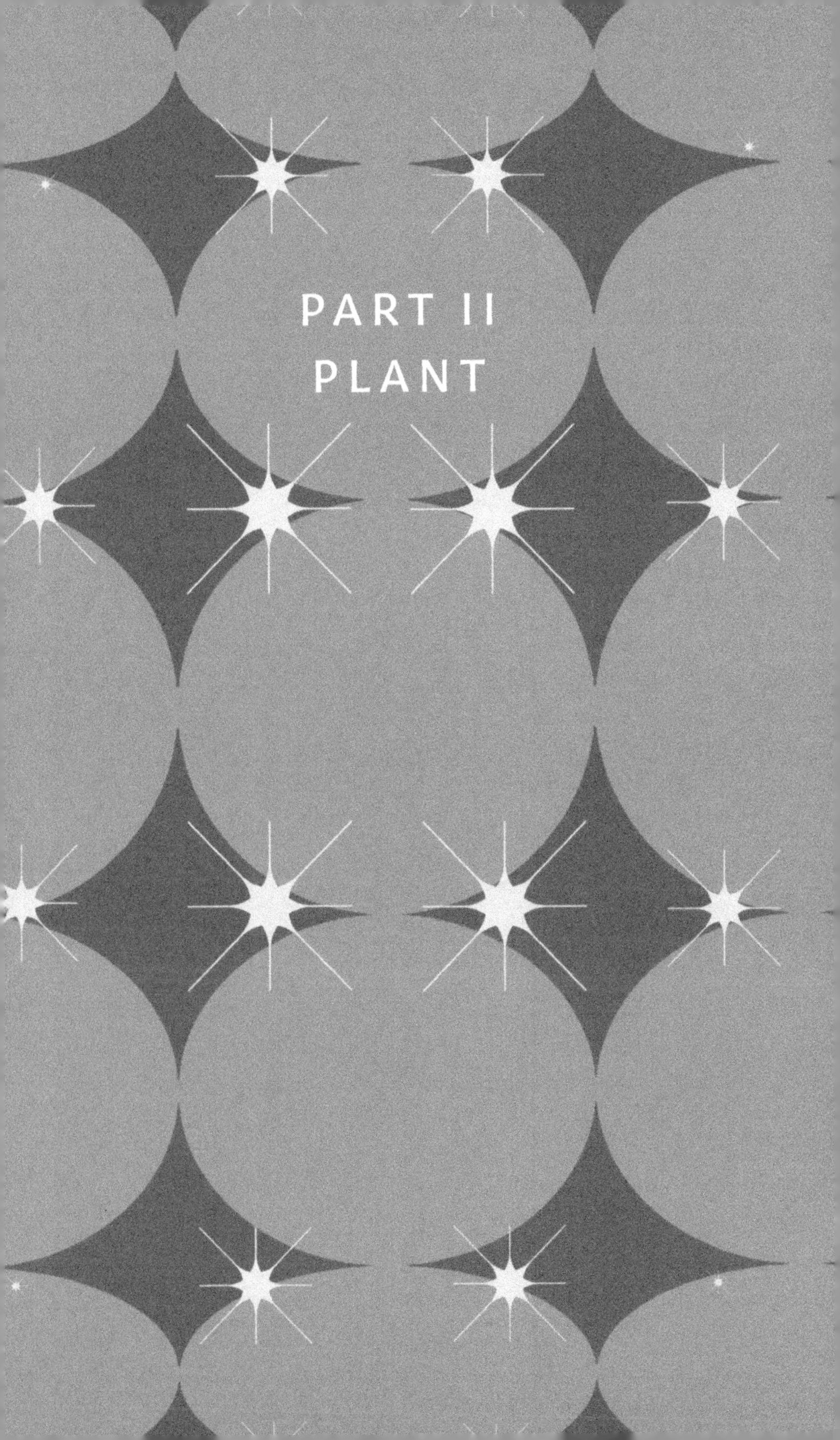

PART II
PLANT

Dirt

If you go back far enough in time, in fantasy, all that's left is dirt. The Bible, and I won't be cracking open a copy just to get this just right, says Adam was made from dirt. Sandy or clay-filled, anthracite-dotted or marshy? Don't know. Plant a few seeds in your palm. See what grows.

Or get one of those DNA-analysis-by-mail kits. At-home simplicity: spit in the tube, seal up the tube, mail back the tube—you're French. Debbie ordered one. Debbie's mother was orphaned as a child. Although she knew the names of her grandparents, a lack of old-timey family photos kept Debbie digging for a where to come from. Debbie's mother was born in a small southern Tennessee town. Debbie's grandmother died shortly after childbirth. Her grandfather was the town drunk. Several of the public intoxication charges on his record are encrypted attempts to have somewhere warm and safe to stay on winter nights: jail. But his story is all dirt, information gone rotten. DNA tests clear away that kind of dirt and make room for another kind: the kind that forms good bodies, holds roots, keeps truths.

People who look and talk like me pay to know they're from a little European region. Then we imagine that thousands of miles and hundreds of years of living in North America are reconciled through the purchase of a quaint cheese, an odd little book, a B and B stay in a drafty room somewhere north of London. That's what Debbie was going for, I think, when she paid to dig in the dirt.

I wasn't there, but I imagine she held the test-results letter in her hand and squinted. Hers is a family of squinters. They search into cabinets with their pointed noses leading the charge, brows furrowed and eyelids brought in almost to touch. They are the image of a bespectacled cartoon mouse, or rat, seeking out something. I make these faces in the mirror and I think I look almost inhuman. Certainly ugly. She and I, we are a family of ugly squinters.

I wasn't there, but I imagine she held the letter in her hand and squinted. "Italian." The salad dressing most common in her parents' home had not, to date, been a term of self-identification for Debbie.

I wasn't there, but I imagine she dug her fingers into the paper a little bit. "Huh? Huh?" Befuddled monosyllabics dribbled from between her lips. Debbie's family is not Italian, whatever that might mean, and so for a DNA test to tell Debbie that she was of Italian origin could only perplex. A corporate lab had spun and sequenced protein chains whose configurations might indicate who'd fucked where in the past. Who got married or fell in love isn't recorded in your genes, but fucking sure is. She knew people had fucked in the swaths of dirt that would become England, Scotland, Germany, and then the Appalachian colonies. But no one had fucked in "the Boot." Now this woman was a boot fucker, but she was the only one in the family.

What this dig for roots sought was the confirmation of the presumed: Scots-something. British Isles bastards. Mixed-up in ways that don't matter, in ways that have no consequences. Maybe she'd find out that someone way back was a big muckety-muck in his village. There could be a crest or a motto, but these would only be foil seals of affirmation stuck to her assumptions.

The dirt held other surprises for Debbie. In the 1990s, aided by another technological purchase, she looked for her fortune. The gizmo in question was something like a Weedwacker, the lawn mower's Gatorade-drinking cousin, but it whacked nothing and beeped instead. She held the knobby terminus over some dirt she'd already dug up once before and the device beeped. Beee

BeeeEEEEeee

BeeP

Beeep Beeep BEEEEEEEEEEEP

A few trowel scrapes later, and I was looking down at a dull half-dollar, minted some time before my birth. The metal detector had found it days before, and now she was showing off the detector's prowess. It was the heyday of the eBay auction, when Joe Shmoes traded in attic debris for big money. To my mind, Debbie was waiting in line for an internet-guaranteed windfall.

Several decades later, Debbie signed up for the extra service whereby the DNA testing company connects you to your newly unearthed genetic relatives. Emails began rolling in from Mr. *Di*This and Mrs. That*oglio*. They were elated to greet previously unknown kin. Debbie didn't want to be welcomed. Looking, perhaps, for comfort, she called her sister, Toni.

"Toni, I took one of those DNA tests. 23andMe. It was only ninety-nine dollars, and I figured since Mom's gone, it's a way to stay connected to the family."

I wasn't there. I don't know what she said. I'm making it all up at this point.

"Ooh, well, that's fun." Toni's stock responses rarely fit the situation.

"Yeah, well, I got the thing back today that tells you, you know, if you're German or whatever and how much. It says I'm fifty percent Italian and I'm like, 'I know I eat a lot of pizza but—'" A conjunction disintegrates into a forced laugh, the kind of laugh you laugh when you really need to stay lighthearted, keep things easy.

"Ooooookaaaaaaay." From Toni, protracted, unmoved by the laughter.

"And now I'm getting all these emails from these Italian people telling me they're my second cousin fifteen times removed or whatever. But I don't know how in the hell I'm fifty percent Italian."

"Maybe they mixed up the samples in the lab or something."

"Yeah. I tried to get Carol to take the test, figure out if our results are the same."

Carol is Debbie's sister. They're both Toni's half sisters, and that whole "half" thing matters. Three clusters existed within this family: the children of Carol and Debbie's father from his first marriage, the children of Carol and Debbie's mother from her first marriage, and the children of the final parental union. Proximity to "your dad" and "my mom" were routinely used to triangulate someone in conversation. When particularly angry with each other, Debbie's parents would call each other by the names of their deceased first spouses. Nell became Lois. Burt became Eugene. Family was tense, temporal. Other marriages had been had, children born at the wrong time according to some. Toni, the only child from Nell's first marriage, was routinely reminded that she in particular wasn't *really* a part of the other two family sets.

"Debbie, do you remember the Germanottis?" the outsider asked over the phone.

They weren't called the Germanottis, but I'm picking the names here.

"Remember how they wanted to pay Mom and Dad to adopt you and Carol?"

It's a story I'd heard before, set sometime in the 1960s: a local couple was desperate for children, but not all their body parts agreed to the want. The husband was Burt's coworker in the glass mill, and Burt and Nell happened to have two young daughters. In a way that wasn't particularly unusual for the time and place, the couple offered to buy/adopt Debbie and Carol. Burt and Nell declined, but the couple remained in the family's orbit.

"And then, you've got all those nights after Mom and Dad came back from the bar,"

Here Toni's larynx rolls on behalf of her eyes.

"when any old bum was allowed to come in the house and sleep on the floor. I'm just saying . . . weirder things have happened."

Silence, maybe, from Debbie, who couldn't have liked the suggestion that her real father was any old bum like Mr. Germanotti.

Then, without laughter, maybe the letter still in hand:

"Well, I don't know. I kinda doubt that."

Debbie drew up a whole scheme for who else in the family could be tested, to rule in or out these possibilities. No one complied, and her logic was flawed anyway. Only if her supposedly full siblings got tested could she know the truth, and they didn't seem interested in digging in the dirt. She ordered another test for herself, collected the sample, mailed it back. The second test told her what she expected to hear the first time. She tried to let the Italian families down gently, but triumphantly, I imagine. She wasn't Italian anymore.

She's not Italian, and we've all left Leechburg. I don't believe in God, or I disbelieve as much as I can. In my mind, it's all dirt now, rotted down. Dirt is a temporal negation. A corpse isn't a person; a buried city is a city no more. The dirt is where something returns to the status of "resource," and we dig in the dirt looking for something useful to us, something that has lapsed out of the circulation of the usefully possessed. Things crawl back out too. Dirt isn't just memory or artifacts or family stories—it's anything we can get our hands on. We look to astrological configurations, alma maters, first jobs, first loves for somewhere to put something we call a root.

"Root" is the name for whatever is pulled up when we begin to move; it's put down when the move is over. We go back to this thing when we're uneasy with the paths we've taken or when we're so old that we can feel ourselves becoming dirt. Example: a pop singer from Nashville, whose main demographic has crow's feet, releasing an album of Patsy Cline covers. The root is a root metaphor for something enduring. Metaphor obscures too.

If I were in your home, I would look around to see which plants are along windowpanes or crammed into telephone nooks. Everyone's got a devil's ivy or a monstera these days. Cactuses too. Plants are coming up out of the dirt all the time.

We're not at your home, though, and we've just met here in a book, which is a sort of mud brick—dirt pressed together, rectilinear artificiality. I don't know which plants you know. You'll forgive me, then, I hope, if I go on and on a bit about plants, but I don't want to leave you out. I just spend so much time in the dirt. I've got nothing to say if we don't go digging a bit, pulling up roots, looking at what grows from where.

Imagine you're in a storefront-turned-church-turned-community center. I'm standing at the front of the room, in front of a room full of chairs. The chairs were inherited from the church that went out of business in this very same spot. The lights are dim, and I'm standing at the front of the room next to a projector screen. You probably don't know what I look like, not enough to imagine me, I know, but I don't really know what I look like either. We can work around that. I'm standing next to a projector screen. I'm going to tell you about some plants now. I've got one of those obsolete wooden pointing sticks. An old carousel slide projector hums, and warm plastic finds our noses. I'm wearing something smart in linen; garden colors: heavy greens, sharp tans, crisp yellows. Take a seat. It won't take so long.

In legumes, the group of plants to which beans belong, roots are colonized by mycorrhizae—root fungi. The plant creates nodules within its root tissue and, inside these chambers, exchanges sugar (produced via photosynthesis) for nitrogen (produced by the bacteria). It's a mutually beneficial off-loading of excess goods inside a porous marketplace. The body of the fungus extends out past the nodule, through the dirt, linking plant to plant in a fuzzy white mesh botanists call a "mycorrhizal network." With chemical pulses, the plants float messages to one another along these fungal strands. Threats to one's own kind are signaled, and resources are redistributed to aid juvenile plants.

Threats are signaled, given, made good, through roots. Juglone, a sour-smelling chemical, is part of the tissues of black walnut trees (*Juglans nigra*), from leaf tip all the way down through their underground parts. Exuding from the tree's roots, the juglone enacts allelopathy—the suppression of one plant by another—and slows the walnut tree's competitors. For the walnut, this means more access to water and light. Among vegetable gardeners, juglone from walnut roots is well known for its fatal impact on nightshades—tomatoes, potatoes, eggplants, chilis, tomatillos.

Poisoning will do, if strangulation isn't an option. Crown vetch (*Securigera varia*) has been planted throughout the United States as a "cover crop." Cover crops shade plots of land during the offseason, preventing weeds from germinating and taking root. Part of the legume family mentioned above, crown vetch deposits nitrogen, collected from copacetic bacteria, into the soil. That nitrogen is later available to other sorts of plants, planted in the same spot. It's a standard engagement for plants in the bean/pea family known as *Fabaceae*: grow, put down nitrogen, be tilled under, get replaced by something like a tomato. Crown vetch grips tight to the soil, pressing valuable nitrogen into crevices of dirt for other plants to use up later, but the plant doesn't know its reach. Spreading by rhizomes (which really aren't roots; let's put that aside for now), crown vetch can turn land into a monoculture of feathery green leaves and clover-like purple blooms. Other plants, less accustomed to grabbing, squeezing, fall by the wayside. Having shown its strength, crown vetch is used to prevent soil erosion. In some American states, however, crown vetch is deemed a "noxious weed" for its interminable hold.

Crown vetch roots might give the impression that roots are—by natural rule—an enduring rivet. Feeder roots soundly reject this. An feeder root is a temporary extension of a plant's root network, sent out to detect or test yet-untapped subterranean pockets of air and water. If these resources are found, more feeder roots will be grown to pull what's needed into the plant. If resources are not found, or once they are depleted, the feeder roots die back. These roots are temporary, single-use.

Then there are the roots that won't go away, even if the rest of the plant is already mulch. Anyone who's ever cut down an old tree knows that roots don't dissolve into ghostly memory after the rest of the tree is removed. Instead, they stay in place—for much longer than you or I—taking up space in the soil and preventing new arrivals. For all the new plant growth they block, these severed roots are railroads for fungal entities, abodes for insects.

And then the projection screen goes blank.

The *Opuntia* cactus swells in desert rain, its paddles filling like ungovernable balloons. When the upper paddles' stored water weight exceeds what spiny joints can bear, the paddles fall to the ground. Rootless, they lay, waiting for moisture and temperature to be right. Then new roots, roots they've never had before, form from "pluripotent areole meristems" along the paddle's surface. These bundles of stem cells let plants continually adjust what they grow and where. Meristems don't have to become roots, however. They're undifferentiated stem cells, capable of being other things if environment and genetics call for such. Roots are not guaranteed within them.

An *Opuntia* paddle goes without roots for a while, but dodders (*Cuscuta spp.*) give them up altogether. After germinating, the infantile dodder plant anchors itself in the dirt with a simple root. Then it casts out winding haustoria that seek a host plant. The root-esque, but decidedly non-root, haustoria tap into the stems of nearby plants to gather the chemicals needed for metabolic processes (also known as "life"). Dodders are unable to photosynthesize, to turn light and water into food. Their leaves are mere scales along a stem. Once a dodder plant is securely attached to another plant via the haustoria, the root rots away.

Covering the ground in golden, hay-like mounds, the dodders of southern Arizona prefer, for their food-surface, splays of scarlet spiderling. Who's doing what to whom aside, the two plants combine visually to make something delicate and pleasurable: deep gray-greens of spiderling leaves found along specks of magenta flowers, streaked with summery lines of dodder. In one sense, dodders have given up on the mystery of dirt, on the occult vagaries of making things anew. In another sense, they revel in secondary products, like those of us who drink and stare at canvases splashed with pigment. Dodders don't give in to the guilty stereotype of the magnanimous old oak, lending shelter to many, nor the temporal certainty of the roots we try to have, in dirt we long to hold. I don't think dodders even know we're here.

Roots have an intense physicality and proximity; no "personal space," no opportunity to really disengage or act alone. It's a life of touch and taste, of chemically and physically sensing what is immediately up against it. It's often done without light. In the dark, yes; hidden, no. The plant is not hiding half of itself. Half of the plant is precisely where it needs to be to do what it does.

Yes, in the back of the room, we have a question.

"What about spider plants in jars of water with, like, roots touched by the sun?"

Good, yes, you're on the right track. And orchids—roots in the air, stems hanging onto shaggy trees. It's more apt to say we want roots to be hidden, or we want an image of something hidden, something we'll call "roots."

All these things roots do: feeding, threatening, trying, holding, disappearing. Maybe our root is our mouth, tied up with an empty stomach. We've got an ache for dirt, to eat it in and spit it out. The mouth is mistaken as an origin point too. "Mother tongues" and "first bites." After a harrowing journey, a kiss is planted on home soil. The whole time the plane shook, mouths were dirty with language. Roots and mouths are routes for getting what we want, getting rid of what we don't. Do you know what you want though?

Some part of me still wants to believe we're made of dirt, like Genesis tells us. It bears a kind of everyday logic that if we can become dirt upon death, then we were already dirt in the first place. What we are now is a temporary aberration. We're golems made from the sorcery of our desire. Our mouths are an incompletion, the limit of our magic.

Centuries ago, it was believed that plants assembled themselves from the matter they pulled from the dirt. From the thick rot, thin leaves. It's a wonderful fantasy, this idea that the energetic essence of nature would unfold itself from tiny plans. More than just the science of DNA, it's an alchemy: within dirt is the possible path to plant. An early scientist named Jan Baptista van Helmont (1580–1644) doubted this model. He grew a willow tree in a pot for five years, carefully weighing the pot, the soil, and the tree at the start. Five years later, he repeated those measurements and found that although the tree weighed much more, the soil had lost little or no mass. Van Helmont surmised all the weight came from the rainwater he provided to the tree. The water, not the soil, accounted for the plant's growth. Plants, it would turn out, build themselves from light and air as much as anything else, but van Helmont wasn't completely off. The soil, the dirt, the roots aren't all we are. There's a compulsion to return, to fill ourselves with the trivia of origins, the unsteady certainty of histories. Between bites, though, the eye travels, spies out all things fleshy and not yet decomposed.

None of my friends has seen a leviathan swimming in the Kiskiminetas River, but they've all seen my houseplants. My houseplants root in the disintegrated memory of riverside hellions. Yours might grow in the dim candlelight of Orthodox Christmas, or the fryer oil of an ethnic fraternal club. And, then again, they're in none of these places. They're out meeting bees and flies and burning up in a sun too bright.

Some Advice

If I drive from Leechburg, Pennsylvania, away from a metal detector's grave
to Tucson, Arizona, direct, nonstop, no points between,
a brick on the gas,
it's because I need some plants,
live and living, not pressed into memory,
so I can go back, and plant them, and make what's
between, all those bypassed points, a visible depth.

I get to Tucson, open the car door, and it's just a wall of burnt air. I've swallowed the blow dryer. I've eaten the oven. I'm not breathing anymore. I'm going to die here. Minutes after arrival, dead, killed,

oh what a shame she couldn't hold on.

I'm some kind of river thing, a carp or a leviathan, and I just can't be here. I'm looking for sewers to wet my head. I'm looking for a mop bucket to gargle myself back to life.

And then the voice of a bumper sticker booms over the West Coast freeway hum:

"Grow where you're planted."

Other voices say "Kindness" and "Coexist" but I'm hearing "Grow where you're planted." It's hot and nothing means anything. Everything's dried up, it's all jerky, all loneliness and hunger. There are stories here, recent and prehistoric, but I don't know them, don't remember them like I remember Holly's van and a high school next to donuts. You could say anything now and there'd be no echo.

I'm out of the car now, against the heat, standing outside a taco joint, looking at a saguaro cactus, which should not be real. The saguaro is a mile marker timing the movements of Wile E. Coyote and Roadrunner. In its television realm, it's only inches tall. This saguaro, ten feet tall, waiting for something, I don't know what, but not a taco, marking something, not a mile, can't be real. I just keep blinking. Here it is, though, real as me, but faring much better in the heat. *I'm wilting. I'm slouching.*

So, I'm looking at it, and hearing "grow where you're planted," and I'm figuring I've gotta try to grow here, where I'm planted.

Like the saguaro, the big fucking deal of the desert. Monarch: grand, pastiche, bit sad if you think about it too long. It's been there so long. It's gotta have some advice. Creosote, too, a twiggy shrub that's green in spring and brown in summer. When temperatures get too high, its waxy leaves are ditched like the liability they are. *Leaves release water, so much water, and you can't afford that, you can't afford to lose all that water. This is the desert.*

You'll die. Every day, in the summer, on the news, I'm gonna die, and there's some man up in the mountain who went up in the mountain and didn't take any fucking water. Why don't men ever take any fucking water? So they've gotta fly in the helicopter, drive up the Jeep, zip over the drone, and just fucking saturate him so he folds back out, so his desiccated bones plump up. From bouillon cube to cow. And now he's on the news, the evening news, so tough and rugged, and he survived. Not like those namby-pamby pansies in the city. He's a big fucking dude, a man, a whole dude man, a saguaro in his own right, just as long as you keep those helicopters, those Jeeps, those drones, those big ol' water jugs coming at him, keeping him from drying out in his own decisions. Don't you know, he's just growing where he's planted?

"Grow where you're planted." *I'm big mad at that advice, a little dumb mad at that advice. It's advice for big dumb dudes way up mountains planning on getting rescued from themselves.*

* * *

"It's a dry hate." A bumper sticker behind the bar of a Tucson watering hole. It's a riff on the desert-versus-swamp debate: it's a dry heat, not a damp heat.

But a gun in the grocery store is a
gun!
in the!
grocery store!
And 115 degrees is still
o-n-e-h-u-n-d-r-e-d-f-i-f-t-e-e-n-f-u-c-k-i-n-g-d-e-g-r-e-e-s.

What do bumper stickers know? Fucking nothing.

* * *

Everything in the shop smells like chiles and cocoa, and I'm running my fingertips across a pair of socks. They're knitted to look like beans and squash growing among stalks of corn. "Three sisters"—a traditional Native American growing strategy, planting beans, corn, and squash all in one plot. The beans fix nitrogen to the soil. The squash leaves shade the ground and reduce water loss. The corn eats the nitrogen and provides a structure for the beans to grow on. Everybody's got something to do where they're planted. I look for a price tag. I'm only looking at the socks because this is a tiny store and I feel like I've gotta look at something.

$14.99? For something that goes on my feet? No.

Instead, I spin the rack of seed packs. This is the Native Seeds store, just a few blocks up the road from our first apartment in Tucson, where we—Harrison and I—moved in the summer of 2015. Everything's in a strip mall in Tucson, and so is this shop. It's a shady corner storefront, with a sort of terracotta look to the exterior walls. Throw an adobe brick, and you'll hit a fabric shop, a Chipotle, and the only hair salon in town I could trust. Native Seeds specializes in saving and distributing the seeds of crops that are native to the region or which have adapted to the climate: devil's claw, Arizona poppy, tomato, corn, cotton, chile, watermelon, basil. I pick up some packets, hopeful, stupid. I haven't grown anything here yet, just arrived. I don't know how anything works here, and I don't even know it.

Nancy rings up my order and slips a sheet of paper into my bag. A few years later, after I've been volunteering with Native Seeds for a while, Nancy will put a glittery black crow—a Halloween leftover—in the shop's front window. I'll have given her the crow as a gift during a white elephant gift exchange. She defends it from all trades. The crow is a critical sign that I belong, and that someone gets me, gets why sparkly Styrofoam is necessary. I don't know any of that yet, but she's slipping a sheet of paper into my bag. It explains something called "sunken bed gardening."

The ancient "sunken beds" method involves digging garden beds lower than the surrounding land. Rainwater is pulled downward by gravity and the soil is forced to drink. It works to an extent, but when all the soil is so terminally dry, the water spreads thin below ground. More than a ditch is needed. Here the bucket of recommendations for "soil improvement" is emptied:

- *Add compost. It'll hold onto the water for you.*
- *Try moss. It's like compost, only it's completely different.*
- *Ollas, pronounced OY-uhz, terracotta cisterns, buried underground, leaking from all their pores, hidden from solar rays.*
- *All that's old-fashioned. Plastics make it possible to complete a slogan. Tubes, like the kind they use to pump blood in and out of a body, scattered across the garden, dripping at scientifically sound rates.*
- *Mulch, which can be compost, or moss. It can cover an old olla or a new tube. Cover it all up.*
- *Oh, and did I mention compost?*
- *I did?*
- *Buy more.*

You must create a temporary, hyperlocal new soil. It's not so much grow-where-you're-planted as plant-a-where-for-you-to-grow.

In our case, any sort of bed sinking or ditch digging required the consent of our landlord, Karen. She knew all about water but never told, kept all its secrets. She'd moved to Tucson from the Northeast with plans to become a hydrologist, but here she found the allure of real estate. We knew all this before meeting her. It was on her blog, alongside entries about local cultural events and her on-the-market properties. She was a real Arizonan, the kind who doesn't fight the climate. Loose clothes, a short bob, anything to keep the air moving. I emailed her a detailed map of where I planned to dig and how I planned to add water to the beds when rain was not forthcoming. She told me I could go ahead, but

"If it damages my property or others,' you'll be legally responsible."

and

"If your water usage increases, I'll increase your rent."

and

"If you've never been afraid to garden, that's about to change."

I dug carefully, distributed water parsimoniously. I've never liked the word "parsimonious," which sounds like a state of being for an old parsnip with glasses who's mad at the paperboy for being late. I do not like it. And I don't think I've ever used it before. And I definitely didn't use the hose. That was Karen's other law: don't water the garden with the hose.

We were only authorized to use the hose once. It was a midnight authorization, an extreme case. Karen appeared at our door late at night, face splattered with mud.

"Would you mind watering those cactuses?"

We'd been watching her for the past half hour as she planted a row of *Opuntia* and ocotillo along the property line, about twenty-five feet from our door. A strange van had driven up our driveway and parked across from our living room windows. Two dark figures emerged from the van, clad in work clothes. It was Karen and a man, maybe her boyfriend. They pulled potted plants from the cargo bed and started digging spots to plant them.

I'd seen Karen earlier that same day, parking her red sedan in the same spot where the van now was. Our neighbor, Molly, was having bricks delivered but didn't have alleyway access to her own backyard. She asked me if she could have the delivery truck come through our driveway and if she could cut through the old wire fence that separated the properties. I told her I was just a renter, gave her Karen's phone number. I don't know what they said to each other on the phone, but the conversation couldn't have been a diplomatic landmark. A few hours later, Karen's car was chucking up dust as it pulled onto the property. She knocked at our door, asked me if I'd spoken to Molly. I said I had and that I'd admitted my lack of authority in the situation. Minutes later, two cop cars parked next to Karen. Everyone took lots of photos, got back in their cars, drove off.

Now Karen was back but with the law in her own soiled hands. She didn't know who owned the old fence, and she wasn't clear on whether or not she could deny Molly access to the driveway. What she did know was that Molly had no legal right to move anything owned by Karen, and Karen could own plants, could plant plants where she wanted, like right along the property line, right where a delivery truck would go and

"If it damages my property or others,' you'll be legally responsible."

In between cactus nodes, she stuffed "NO TRESPASSING" signs.

The cactuses and ocotillo became our responsibility, though not legally. With all proper authorization, we uncoiled the hot rubber daily, turned on the spigot, and directed everything toward the new plantings. They died all the same. It was summer and you can't plant anything, in Tucson, in summer, not even the sturdy cactus.

Grow where you're planted, unless the soil's wrong or the sun's too high. In those cases, give up, dry out, become part of a sign that says "Hey, you, can't you read?"

Without a continuing hose authorization, I was at the mercy of the weather. I put seeds in somewhat evenly spaced holes and sprinkled water from a watering can onto my sunken beds. I waited for winter rains to begin. When they did, I watched from a living room window as my sunken beds filled with liquid and then poured over. Compost, seeds, seedlings flowed out and onto the undug, gravel-covered driveway. The soil was too dry to absorb the water as quickly as it came. The seedlings' roots were too shallow to resist the flow. I was gardening all over, but nothing would come of it.

Tucson is a diagonal line, pressed from the side by hot winds, pressed down by intermittent deluge. The diagonal is the line of sight of a lizard who lifts her head to glance at the edge of an *Opuntia* cactus paddle and up into blue oblivion. It's the diagonal downslope to urgent riverbeds calling for all wandering moisture. It's the diagonal of ocotillo, a plant formed for the heretic's mortification, sticks ringed with unafraid thorns coming from a cluster base and sloping exponentially up to the sun. Eventually, the water arrives, follows the diagonals. Nobody is ready and the city floods, minutely and everywhere. All these lines move things to the extremes which are Tucson: the impenetrable limits of solar annihilation and ephemeral drowning.

Creosote is the shrub that gives the summer air its smell. It lives for millennia in clonal circles. Its brittle and waxy leaves tell you how it lives so long, closing itself off inside itself. Waiting for rain. It's difficult to grow creosote from seed. It just grows itself when it hits the right spot and just holds on, sprouting genetic copies of itself right and left.

* * *

Desert globemallow forms thin louvers across the desert Southwest and down into Southern Mexico. Its tangerine petal cups precipitate out of the winter rains, then disappear as hot summer approaches. How fast are its roots from which telescopic stems form temporary tents? Another local, brittlebush, grows in fluffs of dusty green and sends cool yellow flowers skyward on antenna-like stems. Flowers reach, then dry, then fall as the brittle stem gives in to wind or the passing creature.

Along these plants, haphazardly classified as "natives," were weeds. Like me, they just came along on boats or tire treads from other corners of the world where they'd been more relevant. Some were cached away in the pots of other plants as invisible germs or indecipherable sprouts. These are the cheese-weed mallow, the wild arugula "London rocket," the puncture vine. To scientists, puncture vine is known as *Tribulus terrestris*—a curse on the earth. These plants did what the saying says: they grew where they were planted. They were not Tucsonans like the ones I knew, visiting grandmothers in Barrio Hollywood and Christmasing with cousins in Sahuarita. They had no knowledge of lost Chinatowns, silver mines, the selling of the Southwest to East Coast retirees.

Dandelions weren't as common as I might've liked but were still present around town. Illustrations of dandelions circulate online with captions reminding us that dandelions can widen sidewalk cracks and grow in the joints of a retaining wall. They're a symbol of tenacity, of pulling yourself up by your bootstraps but certainly not by your roots. The advice is to be like a dandelion, who just toughs through, and not like a little sensitive, faggy rose. I've never seen a dandelion punch up through unbroken pavement, though. I've never seen one puncture a passing 737 with spiked leaves. I've never seen one erupt through the stage of a presidential debate, though this would finally give me a reason to tune in. No, I think the inner strength of the dandelion is overstated. It has its limits.

In soft spring mornings, I would "thin" the weeds around my apartment. Traditionally, "thinning" refers to decreasing the number of sprouts for a plant you want—say, tomatoes—increasing the remaining sprouts' access to water, air, and soil. The removed sprouts aren't bad, and it's lamentable that you must kill them, but not everyone can grow where they're planted.

Thinning can be contrasted to "weeding," which pulls up whole stands of plants indiscriminately, as though they were crumbled cans roadside. Weeding removes weeds so that something else called "plants" can grow. All this relies on knowing a plant from a weed and, in Tucson, I did not. Sure, I'd planted some packets of seeds, watched them float away, but there were scores of green things popping up without my planning, without Karen's approval.

I gave individual specimens of prickly, almost dusty Palmer amaranth room to become so tall that they began to curve back down to the earth like a needle completing a stitch. Another name is used for this plant: "carelessweed." London rocket grew in the sun so long that it became too bitter to eat: a mechanism many mustard relatives utilize to deter predators while producing seeds. The name "London rocket" supposedly comes from the plant's quick appearance in the aftermath of the 1666 Great Fire of London. Pendulous flower clusters, creamy yellow, stood atop the London rocket's rickety stems.

Plants often look like they're about to break or snap, but I think that's because we do not understand their flexibility. They cannot run from wind; they must face it. But my bones are jointed (a problem with vertebrates) and when the wind comes, it's me who snaps and runs and thinks the inevitable evaded.

One afternoon, I returned from work, walked up the driveway toward the dead *Opuntia* and skyward weeds, but the weeds were missing. Karen had sent landscapers to clean up the property. For hours, laborers had crawled along the ground, ripping up each root plant by plant by plant. What they couldn't pull up was cut down with a sharp tool, then thrown into a metal garbage can. I didn't want to be angry with them. You can't be angry with them. They're working so hard, in all this heat, not getting paid much, and they're just doing their job, they're just doing what Karen told them to do

but I'm crying, no, you're crying! Why are you crying? They're just weeds. They'll grow back. This isn't your property! You don't own this!

NO TRESPASSING

It's not very revolutionary of you to be angry at the working class. It's not very liberatory of you to criticize Latino laborers who are just trying to make a living. It's not very feminist of you to resent a woman's right to landscape.

I'm so disappointed in you.

Get in the trash can.

For a long time, I thought I kind of liked Karen. I needed to think I liked Karen. It can be dangerous to hate your landlord.

* * *

Two years after we left the desert, I'm in my basement in Swissvale. I come across a bumper sticker in a pile of papers. It's bent but glossy.

It's from Native Seeds. The background is glass gem corn—a variety of corn that gives each kernel its own lustrous color.

The text says "Beauty Is Natural."

I throw it in the trash.

Tree of Heaven

There were no Trees of Heaven in my yard. In late 2021, Harrison and I moved back, from Tucson to Swissvale (or is it Pittsburgh?). I keep shuttling between the two cities in my mind—and maybe I'm writing from both at the same time—but in my Swissvale garden, Queen Anne's lace netted the enduring packaging of single-use objects, blown down the street from the nightclub up the block. Wild daisies did things without names. But there were no Trees of Heaven and no room for them. I'd heard a song, and it warned me:

> Now the Tree of Heaven is their preferred host.
> Yeah, that's the tree they like the most.
> So, if you've got one in your yard: chop it down.

The *they* of "their" is the spotted lanternfly: *Lycorma delicatula*. It's a beautiful insect. As a young nymph, its geometric body is a starry sky. As it ages, red like a salivating mouth appears on its exterior, and its leg joints are dotted white. In its adult form, it's a strawberry shortcake polka-dot blur that jumps from sidewalk to wall to plant. Coming to Pennsylvania from China, perhaps via boat, spotted lanternfly has no natural predator in these parts. It drinks sap unreservedly from the vines of grapes and hops and, maybe, clematis. The USDA, along with other such entities, views spotted lanternfly as an agricultural pest.

Agricultural pests are creatures who can collapse farms, bankrupt communities, and produce food shortages. It's somewhat avoidable suffering. I should avoid it and avoid making it. That's precisely why I don't have Trees of Heaven in my yard. Spotted lanternflies, the song tells me, like Tree of Heaven the most, so I ban it from my garden. No matter how irresponsible my neighbors may think me to be, with my seven-foot chandeliers of toxic pokeberry and spectacular runs of poison ivy, I draw the line at Tree of Heaven. I must avoid the delicate spotted trouble it invites. Simply not in my yard. No.

Instead, the native sumac has outposts throughout my plot: one toward the front door, one along the side of the house, and one in the back garden. Sumacs have "compound leaves," something many of us associate with tropical foliage. Pointy green extensions ("leaflets") cluster along a single stem, forming a leaf that looks like many leaves, similar to a palm or a fern. In the summer, the sumac's red flower clusters constitute cartoon candle flames, pointy tips to the sky. The fruits, dried and crushed, are a tart note in Levantine cooking, and they can be used for a lemonade-like drink. Sumac is a beautiful tree and a long-standing part of southwestern Pennsylvania's ecology.

When friends visit, I point out my sumacs with more than a little pride. I spotted these native trees through my eager knowledge of plants, assiduously protected them, and kept them growing. Soon I'll be drinking sumac refreshments and offering them to guests like a television character from a *Charmed* × *Martha Stewart Living* crossover. Staghorn sumac forms the red panicles I described, though we of western Pennsylvania are also neighbor to the green-flowered "smooth sumac." I don't know exactly which species is in my yard, but a field guide could tell me.

The Trees of Pennsylvania Field Guide, by Stan Tekiela, is a "famous field guide by an award-winning author," according to the publisher's description. (Note to self: win awards, get famous.) It's a pocket text with a glossy red exterior and "gee-whiz tidbits" from Stan. The back cover says Stan will help me "decide between look-alikes." It's a trade: to learn about a plant from other people, I have to give up the mystery of what it *could* be. If I want to know how a plant will grow in five years, what color its flowers might be, if it's edible or ready to kill—all without waiting or dying—I have to rely on someone else's observations. To use those observations, I have to have the tree's name—preferably, its botanical name. A botanical name is a two-part coordinate that's an encrypted shorthand for all sorts of knowledge. Once a plant's botanical name is known, the identities of its relatives can be guessed. The structure of its flowers can be anticipated without having ever seen a bud. Visiting pollinators can be imagined. A calendar unfolds, coordinating the experience of a plant with the timing of seasonal fluxes. Through a botanical name, you can confirm your own knowledge, become your own, new Stan. In exchange for this knowledge, some of the ability to be surprised by a plant must be surrendered. The joy of being perplexed by an unnamed, unknown plant is abbreviated.

To find out whether my sumac would simmer green or burn red, I opened Stan's famous guide and flipped to the index, looking for "Sumac." Three entries:

Sumac, Poison
Sumac, Smooth
Sumac, Staghorn

Poison sumac looks nothing like the other two, so I'd ruled it out already. I was hoping for the third: stunning, smoky, hungry staghorn sumac. I turned to page 251, the entry for *Rhus typhina*. *Trees of Pennsylvania* describes the staghorn sumac's serrated leaflets, its soft bristles along the stem. Though out of season, it describes the flower clusters and fruits I wanted to see. My sumac was a little different, with hairs too small for the eye to resolve. The edges of its leaves were smoother than Stan or I expected. This happens when identifying plants. They're always more complicated than guidebooks suggest. For instance, mulberry trees often have leaves of multiple shapes on a single plant at a single time—some rounded, some lobed, some looking like a flame in need of a hug. Plants are living things, and they respond to what's around them. They are not made in factories of certainty.

I thought perhaps the smooth leaflets could be a sign that this was a smooth sumac, not a staghorn. A disappointment of sorts, and I flipped to page 249. Page 249 told me that it's not the leaves of smooth sumac that are smooth but the branches. My smooth-leafed sumac remained indistinct, unresolved along two sharp images.

Having only two options is the basis of a botanist's dichotomous key. A dichotomous key asks either/or questions in an ever-narrowing progression toward one answer. All other answers are excluded on unclimbed branches along the way. The questions start with big, broad impressions—like whether the plant is a tree, a shrub, or a vine. Then they move inward until you find yourself counting bits of a flower, or finding *stipules*: leaflike blurbs at the base of a leaf stalk. (Go search the plants around you for something green and wordless where a leaf meets a stem. Find a stipule.)

Tekiela's *Trees of Pennsylvania* doesn't present a dichotomous key exactly but gives a truncated version: Is the tree an evergreen or deciduous, with leaves leaving in the fall? Either way, next come questions about leaf shape and arrangement. These questions translate the amateur's image of a plant into the anatomical grammar of botany. Following Stan's simple key, I could describe my unknown sumac as having compound, alternately attached leaves. The entries for those sorts of trees began on page 227. Here or somewhere afterward, I'd gather the name of my sumac.

I couldn't use Stan's book to describe a Tree of Heaven. The top is impossible to see. Its trunk reaches heights of three hundred or four hundred feet. Its leaves are a lace of photosynthetic Lucite discs forming an indistinct canopy. Which bit of green attaches to which stem is indecipherable. Branches are only seen if sought. Its flowers are pushes of heady pink, sloped by the heel of a palm. Smell them, lose your balance and your words and not want them back. Bark the color of coffee with two tablespoons of cream. Deep roots. There are no clouds in the sky.

When the song told me to cut down the Tree of Heaven, I was living in Arizona, and I'd never even seen this plant. They must've been there, though. Tree of Heaven is credited with saving Jerome, Arizona, a small town threatened by mining-induced land instability. In the 1960s, Tree of Heaven was planted so its "aggressive" roots might keep the dirt from skidding about. I never went to Jerome, though, and nobody ever pointed at a tree in Tucson and said, "That's a Tree of Heaven!" Even if they had, I wouldn't have believed them. I'd seen it in my mind, and it couldn't grow on this earth. On earth, Tree of Heaven was a sound, a mouth shape.

I had no eyes for Tree of Heaven; they were filled with "Devil's Thorn," alternately called puncture vine, goathead, and caltrop. It stays close to the desert ground, sending stems from a central point and covering a patch of land with tiny green leaves and buttercup-like blossoms. Fertilized flowers form "achenes"—hard, nutlike fruits with several spines—about the size of a clove. The achenes quickly fill the gaps in a sneaker's tread. Bike tires are flattened. Dog paws assailed. Some plants rely on animals to eat their fruit and pass along the seeds. Dandelions throw them off on a breeze. Devil's Thorn stabs in, takes a blood meal when it can. It insists on being seen.

Don't leaves of morning glory look free, slipping up an oak branch in July sunlight? They move and they aren't afraid of falling. They don't know falling. They don't climb a tree with the intention of coming back down. On the way up, they become everything they need to stay forever. That's what a saint is, I think. Saints are florid glows of living on the way up an oak. Katharine Hepburn said she wanted to be an oak, if she had to be a tree. It was a silly question Barbara Walters once asked her:

and I'm paraphrasing
"Ms. Hepburn"
again, not a quote here,
"what kind of tree would you be, if there were a decree that to be, then a tree you must be?"

Hepburn said she'd be an oak. I think Walters got her question from a joke book or something like that. Totally unserious. She was just flipping through the pages in her green room, picking out anything. Heaven only knows what a book might contain.

On page 227 of Stan's tree guide began the listing of trees with compound, alternately attached leaves—trees like the one a few feet from my face, like the sumac in my yard that I needed to name. Entry one: Common Hoptree? No. Entry two:

faux vernis du japon, also known as,
臭椿, also known as,
ghetto palm, also known as,
Tree, but of Heaven, but also known as,
"Tree? Heaven and that's from whence it derives," said by someone who's the fourteenth baronet of something, which is also known as,
A tree for angel food cake, also known as,
Afterlife's arborescence, eternally also known as,
Good people's branches.

Have you ever refused to know? Of course you have. It's a rhetorical question. Some weather you're having.

A medium tree of "single, or multiple crooked trunks," Tree of Heaven has compound, alternately attached leaves, just like the trees in my yard. Its bark is a light brown, and some describe it as having the texture of cantaloupe skin. Its leaflets are smooth except for two teeth—little bumps on either side of the leaf's base. The underside of those teeth shows glands that look like blisters or papules. The leaves smell like old vegetable oil that was once used to fry peanuts.

Tree of Heaven looks very much like the tree that was in front of me as I stood guide-in-hand asking Stan to tell me, "It's a sumac." It looks very much like the trees I'd pointed out to friends, trees I'd made into promises of hospitality.

Before Stan's book, sumac could grow in my yard. The space where Tree of Heaven might take root was clear, and the sour native poured in. I couldn't see Tree of Heaven. I couldn't know it when I saw it. An invasive species of "aggressive" roots and unpalatable company couldn't be in my yard. No. I saw what I knew how to see—native sumac. A native species has a right to grow, a reason to grow. It is part of ecological webs and networks of good living. It's all the stuff that was better before we touched it with our eyes-like-cameras. Organic, wholesome, and cooperative. A tree of life, like the sumac, has a clear meaning. Tree of Heaven is a plant from elsewhere. It says what I fear has already happened. I've already seen heaven.

I shouldn't have to remind anyone, but "thou shalt not make unto thee any graven image, or any likeness of any thing that is in heaven above, or that is in the earth beneath, or that is in the water under the earth." It's part of that list: "10 Easy Ways to Keep God from Killing You in the Desert." We can skip around the second half of the edict, assuming no plagues will come as a result of our cat tchotchkes and singing-fish plaques. An image of heaven is too close to the start of the sentence though. We couldn't have missed that part. It's pure rebellion to see heaven from here. A Tree of Heaven shouldn't be here, if we're playing by the rules. A Tree of Heaven on earth means the rules are over.

Seeds from the Tree of Heaven have fallen from a place that is a promise and a threat. That's what heaven is, I think, a threat. Do everything right and get chucked up there, right next to the guy who played judge my whole life. And what am I supposed to do for all eternity, but worry that I'm the next Lucifer, on my way to getting kicked out for being a little too happy to hear my own voice? Tree of Heaven makes heaven close enough to be a trouble, a "What do I do about this?" There's no safety later, no safety now.

And now, I've failed to make an unquestionably good, native garden. I've failed to look at, without touching, a pure "before things went wrong." The Trees of Heaven and spotted lanternflies are already here. Here is already there. Place is dissolving.

Today is 1740, and Jesuit priest Pierre d'Incarville is shipping himself from France to Beijing via Macao. Like other whites in China, d'Incarville wanted to save Chinese souls and fire European economies. The latter would be done through the careful selection, propagation, and use of plants found in Asia. The Chinese varnish tree (*Rhus verniciflua*, its botanical pseudonym) was of commercial interest to Europeans, who coveted the high-gloss sap of this sumac species. During travels through the Lower Yangtze region, d'Incarville encountered *Rhus verniciflua*—more or less. Shiu Ying Hu words it perfectly in her canonical essay for the journal *Arnoldia*: "When he was in the Lower Yangtze Region, he observed the Chinese varnish tree (*Rhus verniciflua*), apparently from a distance. After settling in Peking, he began to study the plants, collect specimens and seeds, and ship them to Paris. On seeing the ailanthus [Tree of Heaven] in Peking, he assumed it to be the varnish tree of the Yangtze Region and sent the seed of ailanthus to Paris with a note about the lacquer tree."

Apparently from a distance. D'Incarville was nearsighted in the eyes, maybe, or in the mind. Somehow, he couldn't see Chinese varnish tree clearly. He had a brief impression and saw it elsewhere, including where *ailanthus*, Tree of Heaven, might have grown. When he returned to Beijing, he pointed out trees that matched this impression and gave them the name he wanted them to have—Chinese varnish tree.

From Paris's Jardin Royal des Plants, seeds from d'Incarville's trees were sent to England and grown at the Physic Garden at Chelsea, among other places. In 1784, William Hamilton brought seeds to Philadelphia for planting at his Woodlands estate. Everyone was growing their lacquer trees in the plush of nature when, in 1785, R. L. Desfontaines published *Mémoire sur un nouveau genre d'arbe*, Ailanthus glandulosa. *Mémoire* argued that nobody was growing varnish-producing sumac trees, not if they got their seeds via d'Incarville. They weren't growing any kind of sumac at all. Desfontaines writes, "We've had this tree in our gardens for quite some time. Until now, it's been taken by most botanists to be *Rhus succedanea* or *grand vernis du Japon* [Chinese varnish tree] because no one had yet observed the flowering, and its leaves have a remarkable resemblance to those of *Rhus succedanea*. . . . The description that I will give of it will show that, not only is this tree not *Rhus succedanea*, but that it's a genus very different from that of *Rhus* or sumacs" [translation mine].

Put more simply, no European had seen d'Incarville's Beijing-born varnish tree bloom. Desfontaines was the first, and what he saw was d'Incarville's mistake. Linnaean plant classification, the sort made of dichotomous keys and Stan's guides, is ever focused on the reproductive tidbits of a flower. Arrangements of floral parts, perhaps more than anything else, form the scientific identities of plants. Desfontaines says no flowers had been seen by d'Incarville and others, meaning an undeniable identification had not been possible. D'Incarville saw something *from a distance*, and no hand lens could get any of the growers any closer. Wishing stayed supple, possible. Until Desfontaines came along, Chinese varnish tree spread from Beijing to Paris to England to Philadelphia. Once Desfontaines saw the flowers on the varnish tree, a different tree began to appear in those plots: *Ailanthus altissima*—Tree of Heaven.

Tree of Heaven was already established on at least three continents by the time Desfontaines made that distinction. On the East Coast of the United States, Tree of Heaven was appreciated for its rapid growth, even if varnish wasn't forthcoming. It grew well in polluted urban environments and provided deep shade with its dense canopy. Slower-growing native trees, accustomed to unimpeded sunlight, were now withering in the same shade for which Tree of Heaven was lauded. Its allelopathic roots sent toxic compounds to struggling neighbors. It dropped tens of thousands of seeds and summoned clones to sprout from the soil below.

Less than two hundred years after it was brought to America, writers were describing Tree of Heaven as a weedy nuisance. It outcompeted many other species for resources and was a considerable challenge to uproot. Once championed for its urban tenacity, it was now a sign of a ghetto—a place where nothing of any worth would grow. Certainly not a sumac.

We thought we had varnish, then we didn't. We wanted shade, then we didn't. We dreamed of strong roots, but we didn't have them and didn't know what to do with them when Tree of Heaven brought them our way. Even Jerome, Arizona, which owes its continuance to Tree of Heaven, is trying to uproot it. "Tree of Heaven" became the name of a plant no longer visible in the shade of our unruly wants. We keep covering things up, then getting mad that we can't see clearly. We don't want to see clearly, I'm here to tell you.

I go into nature, which is a way of saying I drive a few hours south of Pittsburgh and stay with city friends in the house they're renovating. The open field of coneflower, milkweed, ironweed, and yarrow slips me under the soil, and I'm dirt. I'm earthy and endless, I start to believe. More honestly, I am still the small, neurotic me, but I'm seeing each bloom as an extension of my desire. I'm tricked by the hope of escaping the life of today, in a world crisscrossed by the sending of seeds and bodies and poisons and varnish. I'm wanting that untouched before, that really knowable me. A "me" untouched by circumstances. So many vague visions have gone unfulfilled. I'm trying to make up for them with a botanical name, a set of coordinates, a scientific point of view that can turn my unclear visions into authoritative sight.

I get back to the city, and I remember that I'm not a knowable *thing*, distinct from others. I'm a path for all that shipping. I'm saturated by the trouble of plants without clear meanings, and me without roots. You might read this from your farm and think you are different, but I have to be honest and tell you: I don't think you are. The desire to find peace in an open field is the desire to find peace in the past, is the desire to find salvation in China, is the desire to die, go to heaven, and never feel the hunger of desire again.

I come back from Beijing and Paris and Philadelphia to my garden in Swissvale. Letters arrive out of time from Desfontaines. He tells me the tree I thought I'd seen is really an outgrowth of vision's limitations. I saw it from a distance. "There are Trees of Heaven in your garden," Desfontaines continues. Now, I wonder if I have to do what the song says: "Chop 'em down."

It's probably better to dig them up though. No matter how it's cut down, it regroups in the roots and sends up new stems, sometimes several feet away. If you want Tree of Heaven to vacate the premises, you've got to rip it out from where it is. You have to take away the where of its growing.

I make it go elsewhere, back underground or into a garbage heap. I dig up my Trees of Heaven, save for one that is too close to a garden fence. I trim that one back periodically. Two years after arriving in Swissvale, my lone Tree of Heaven is dotted with spotted lanternflies in their second nymph stage. Additional garden guides tell me to spray the tree with an organic pesticide. Others suggest I begin to systematically poison the tree so the lanternflies will die as they devour. Always, there is something to fix.

I go elsewhere instead, like the city pool. A few blankets away, some people who don't remember me are playing house music on a portable speaker. Conversations are half-heard. Whistles are blown for illegal flips. When I learned to swim, I was afraid of slipping beneath the water, of the water reaching into me. And then I'm gone, lost from my thin atmosphere. I'm something else, like a corpse or a cautionary tale. I lose the trace of my origin. I become someone else's bad feeling.

Instead, I go elsewhere, like a little café in the neighborhood next to mine. I type up some things about Tree of Heaven. I look across the café patio and see something growing out of a tall lapis planter. It has compound, alternating leaves. Smooth with teeth at the base. I get up and walk over to the plant. I rub the leaves and smell my hands. Old oil used for frying peanuts. They're growing Tree of Heaven like a palm or a sumac.

Now that spotted lanternfly is here, "Tree of Heaven" isn't just the name of a something-to-be-fixed. Used to be, things were fixed by removing the Tree of Heaven, removing the invasive species from the "where" of its growing. The arrival of spotted lanternfly has turned Tree of Heaven itself into a "where"—a place from which to be removed, a way to uproot an insect. Tree of Heaven is falling into the shade of an organism much smaller, an organism that eats our food before we can. All this is predicated on forgetting where Tree of Heaven was seen "apparently from a distance"—China. In China, Tree of Heaven is a source of traditional medicine, wood for steaming trays. It's referred to as a "spring tree" because it's the last tree to swell its buds. When they swell, you know you've really made it through winter. You're still living.

If Tree of Heaven grows too fast and spreads too far, is too shady, and is feeding our foes, then it has to be said that it's doing all those things *here*. In her essay on the tree, Hu remarks that Americans never really figured out how to live with Tree of Heaven. Not as pliant as a pine, Americans called it too wild and lamented planting it here.

In eyes like mine, Tree of Heaven was a wish for lacquer. In cities like mine, it was a wish for shade and green leaves. For me, it was a wish for the pleasure of friends. It was a wish to make my sourness lovable. For ecologists, Tree of Heaven is covered in red-spotted wishes for a time before we wished. It's regret, and that's a terrible thing to make out of another life.

Or What Heaven Can't See

From the bottom of the basement stairs, I looked up. I didn't know if my mother would make it downstairs in time to survive, in time to take each step slowly. The staircase was malformed. The treads were too shallow to hold half a human foot, and the raisers too short. Scrubby, hostile carpet had been tacked along the flight. It was so easy to tip forward, fall onto concrete with only a laundry basket for comfort. The whole house was a bit handmade, in the worst way. Now, my hand was wrapped around an aluminum can, which I hoped would feed me for a week. I hoped my mother would bring another can or two with her, would get downstairs before the computers crashed and the bombs went off. We'd never survive unless we hid with our few canned vegetables. We'd wait until . . . *until what*?

I wasn't sure when or how our salvation would come. The men on the television had been clear about the chaos en route but less clear about how it would be resolved. Some preachers claimed that God would teleport the faithful aboard heaven. There we would close our eyes in worship and close our eyes to the evisceration of the wretches left on a sinking, burning earth. Perhaps we'd be evacuated before I could turn the crank on the can opener. Or perhaps we'd be left on earth just long enough for me to hear my spoon scrape the bottom of each can. A trial of faith would be my ticket. Afraid of being left behind, forgotten, or too weak to endure: New Year's Eve, 1999.

Twenty years later, and I'm waiting, similarly panicked, on a midcentury modern sofa. It's not Y2K but another string of buzzy letters. A pandemic began, somewhere at some time, and I think we're still living inside it. How long it will stretch and whether we are at the beginning, middle, or end is unknowable. We didn't even know *this* would happen. In what were hopefully the early nights of it all, I waited in my living room. The light of two table lamps was softened across grains of dust resting on fabric, glass, and metal. For animals other than we who wait, nights are full of dust. People who wait are always trembling a little, keeping the motor running so we can shoot off at the first sign of "the right time." The dust can't rest on us. Nothing to see, not yet, so I wait.

In superstitious times, waiting is a pivot. We choose to wait or we choose not to wait. We act or we hold our breath. Me, I wait. I stay quiet to go unseen. When I think of choosing *not* to wait, I hear tender joints wrapped in thin skin rapping against particleboard covered in a wood-print laminate; I see salt thrown to flavor the ground we kiss; I hear fossilized phrases half-muttered and almost wholly unheard.

My early pandemic nights were spent sitting up in the living room, waiting.

Early in my life and early in the Bible came the story of the Exodus. Synopsis: God tells the descendants of Abraham, Isaac, and Jacob that he'll get them out of this whole "Egyptian slavery" thing. *Finally, right?*

Here's the catch: he's going to blow through Egypt and murder every firstborn creature of every species. Is he cracking a crème brûlée with a jackhammer? Yes, he is. The Israelites and their comrades will be spared but only if they move with precision: slaughter a young lamb, place its blood on the doorposts, eat its meat with bitter herbs, wear shoes through the meal, lock the doors, wait in their houses until daybreak. They can't wait to do some things, must wait to do others. If they failed to orient themselves to waiting in this contradictory way, their futures would be closed to them. On that night, death lingered in Egypt until it was exhausted, until God lost interest in the game. Death is not a threat here but a lure, an enticement.

Do it!

No, wait!

Wait, now, move!

Wait, no, wait, hold still, no!

In another desert, this instructing voice hitched a ride on my own breath. I spoke it to myself, as though it were a spell. I marked myself with the devices of salvation as dictated to me by a hostile trace of religious education. I tried to be *good.* I tried to wait and rush in the right configuration, to blend into God's pattern. Nothing to see.

The vestigial organs of my mind secrete an unsteady definition of "good": Good is *luck.* Good is pleasing God, which is a matter of luck. It's not straightforward. Predicting the correlation between my actions and God's pleasures is futile. The fibrous scabs threaded across his psychic wounds might catch on the slightest of my movements and provoke a rage I anticipate but for which I can't really prepare myself. All the while, he's up there grinning and chanting the song of a cross-wired stoplight. In place of science, a new law: every action is forbidden from having equal or opposite reactions.

If pleasing God is good, then displeasing him, giving him a bad feeling, is sin. This definition creates an unflattering image of God—someone so petty that his experience of distaste equates to universal error. I believe in this God like I believe in crimes I have yet to commit.

What displeased God was a matter of debate in our church. Some in our congregation held that women shouldn't wear pants. Maybe God was worried he wouldn't know men from women if they dressed the same. Or perhaps he's a fan of skirt fabric's float. Anxious or aesthete, your choice, but numerous men in our group were confident that God didn't like ladies in trousers. Many women, understandably, disagreed with this interpretation of his scriptures. Some congregants agreed that God didn't *prefer* women in pants, but he certainly was not repulsed by it. Abortion was a more unifying topic. God was incensed by abortion. It was undeniably a sin, and no disagreements would be tolerated.

Most day-to-day life was more like pants than abortion. My '90s childhood coincided with the prime of *The Power Rangers*—a wholly verboten piece of media in my home. To this day, I can't tell you the premise of *The Power Rangers* or name any of the characters except Rita Repulsa—an enviable name. The Rangers, from the little I knew, did not attribute their powers, which I'm assuming they had, to God. To have any sort of power, and not offer that power up to God as his own, was a sin. I don't know for certain that they even had powers, but I'm certain I wanted powers for them, wished powers onto them. Although they used the powers I gave them to fight something bad, their fight wasn't pure enough to please God. The arrival of *The Power Rangers* onto the television screen, like pants slipped onto women's legs, was a test of one's ability to please him.

No one ever told me to change the channel when the Rangers took over the screen. I did it myself, to and for myself, on behalf of God. A good Christian child does not need sin to be labeled explicitly but responds to an inner sense of what is good. If you believe in sin and God, like I did and maybe too often still do, you can tell very quickly when to change the channel. Change it when the cross can't be seen and the theme song fails to reference the glory of God. Change it when no one's changing to please God.

For all these reasons, I should've changed the channel when Lynda Carter, in between her commercials for Lens Express contact lenses, changed from Diana Prince into a syndicated Wonder Woman. The TV remote was too heavy to lift when I saw her though. I watched her lamé cuffs repel bullets of all sorts in my grandparents' living room. She fought Nazis and communists. I knew what Nazis were. Every Sunday—and most other days—our church prayed for Israel, the nation-state. Though we lacked any accurate knowledge of Jewish culture or religion, Jewish people were held to be an ethnic ideal. From our own God, they'd been given status and distinction. We lacked, too, any understanding of why Jewish people didn't view Jesus as God's second jackhammer, sent to fix everything with more slaughter, this time a bit more melancholic. We simplistically thought they'd rejected him out of a rigid adherence to tribal law. Jewish people were still God's favorite though. We didn't view the Holocaust—the Nazis—as evidence against this. God had experienced displeasure and historical events proceeded from that feeling, the people of my church argued, but firstborn is firstborn. In *Wonder Woman*, a gleaming face, presented as though it were white, streaked the skies in a crystalline airplane. She sought out the Nazis who had outlasted God's anger. These men, lurking Teutonically among the banana trees, were now demons—evil with its own mind. I watched her dazzle her supervisor, played by Lyle Waggoner, with her stain-free demon slaying.

I watched Lyle Waggoner pine after Diana. I pined after both their images. I imagined myself enrobed in how others saw them, how they were understood to be in the world. I pined after the desire that slipped across them. If the Power Rangers got their powers from me, I got mine from *her*. That was her—Diana's, Lynda's, woman's—sin. Though she stopped Nazis, did God's will, she wasn't stopping me and my fantasy of becoming her—all those straight teeth and glossy locks and grins from men.

Television-blasted eyes could never hope to sin as thoroughly as the mouth. The worst sin possible is an arcane speech act known as "blasphemy of the Holy Spirit." What precisely constitutes blasphemy of the Holy Spirit was, like the powers of the Rangers, not very clear to me back then and still isn't. Maybe it's simple disbelief: I don't believe in the Holy Spirit. Or maybe you have to believe but with irreverence: the Holy Spirit is the least popular spirit in the bar. Or do you have to be innovative, naming your dildo "The Holy Spirit?" All the biblical lines about being "filled with the spirit" come to mind, all puns intended. It could be that simple rejection is required: Holy Spirit, I don't want you.

With unfixed dimensions, blasphemy of the Holy Spirit was an obvious and total failing. God would not, under any circumstance, forgive the sinner who found their way to these unknown words. My heart still beats a little faster typing these sorts of things and my eyes shift from the computer screen to a midpoint between me and it. Nothing to see.

The god who cannot forgive blasphemy of the Holy Spirit is the perfect friend, so loyal. Any slight against the one he loves is beyond indulgence. Any flaw in the beloved object is ripped from his looking eye. A pitted, scarred vision makes him unsteady on his feet, reaching for a ghostly hand. He has sacrificed so much to be this fool.

In the apologia of our church, it was said that God made humans so he might have an image of himself, an image he could love. Then the images failed him. I have other thoughts: He made us so his hate might have an object outside himself, so he could stop mutilating himself in the dark. Our failures are the only image God could ever have of himself. Eve failed, ate some fruit, got fruity, and then came all the fiery punishments and flesh-consuming diseases on earth, the recompense for being the image of a god who despises what he made. Displacements.

God Jr. got involved. He felt bad for we embroiled critters and took the bus to earth. He tried to slum it a little, pick up our tabs. A cult started in God Jr.'s name, confessing all the things I just told you about a man in the dark. That's how I know all this. He was crucified and died on our behalf, even though we keep dying and I keep getting electricity bills and the debts keep mounting so high you'd think he could see them.

Christ's Passover melodrama, fortunately, worked on the Father. Now he lets all our foibles pass if we just say we're sorry. At age five, the news of this forgiveness brought me immense comfort. I'd been so bad without knowing it, but clemency was available to me. Then the fine print came into focus: all sins could be forgiven, *except for blasphemy of the Holy Spirit.* Nothing Christ did could close that loophole, though he made no mention of it during his monologue on the cross.

"Father, forgive them, for they know not what they do."

(turning, breaking the fourth wall, in a louder voice, like Donald Trump tacking on something he just thought of)

"Except, of course, blasphemy of the Holy Spirit, which I totally know you can't forgive."

He could forgive the murderer, the child molester, the dog beater, the black-market organ trader, the man who doesn't care what he looks like. He could not forgive what I had discovered. When or where I learned about this "unforgivable sin" is lost to me. Maybe that gap in my memory can testify to the shock this knowledge brought. In that lost moment, I discovered a sin so severe that even God was slack-jawed by its depravity. My flesh felt cold on the bone and I became dizzy. Tears came close. I would do it, I knew it. I would blaspheme the Holy Spirit. Or maybe I already had? Would I know?

The punishment for this unforgivable sin was unimaginative—hell. Down there, a woman who had an abortion shrieked as bloodied toddlers tugged at her fingers. The teen who'd fucked too soon, before the wedding rings were on, underwent the forced caresses of a hag-like demon. A really nice old lady was crumpled on the ground, with joint pain even where joints hadn't been. She never got around to "getting saved," to asking God for forgiveness. Crime enough. Everywhere, fire burned the nerves and left skin undamaged.

Hell wasn't death, but the chasmic capacity of life gone terribly wrong. All appearances of "death" were actually continuances of living forms. Nothing actually ends. You go *somewhere*, whether that's heaven or hell. You endure or bask in *something*. There is no disappearance from existence. No limits. Nothing to see there. The afterlife is perhaps meant to be a comfort, but this attachment to life is tensed like the jaws of a dog locked onto the leg of another animal. It rips the flesh, brings horror, turns each blink eternal. Whatever is now is forever.

Heaven was impossible to depict, but my church attempted an infernal *tableau vivant* several years in a row. Titled "Hell House," the performance was ordained as a godly alternative to October's Halloween festivities. Concerned to eradicate all traces of paganism—introduced into the faith by eclectic Catholics—these righteous Protestants abolished the molded-plastic pumpkin bucket, the cat-ear headband, and the brad-jointed paper skeleton. Most children in the congregation didn't go trick-or-treating. Those who did left their candy exploits uncelebrated. Better not to speak of the joy. All these festive excesses pushed death beyond a cold threat toward something worn and warm, something that burned with anticipation.

Volunteers hung velveteen curtains from the ceilings of our storefront-turned-church, dividing the space into vignettes of damnation. A congregant who owned an electronics store provided red lights and fog machines. Hell House attendees would transit openings in the curtains to see church leaders posed as damned sinners. The worship leader was an adulterer, putting her vocal training to use in worrying bellows. The deacons were demons, hassling visitors between stops. They all screamed out their isolation—forever separated from God, their families, their friends. No one could see or hear their suffering. They were trapped inside themselves, so they grabbed the arms of those who walked by, who sought to ignore them. At the end of the line, someone, maybe the pastor, was positioned to corner the visitors, give them as much good news of salvation as they could stand. If I blasphemed the Holy Spirit, whatever that meant, I'd go to this hell forever. I'd be alone, forever, with only some kind of unsympathetic, taunting imp for company. The imp would look like someone I know.

As I walked through Hell House, the kids from my school and neighborhood came to mind. They weren't like me, in the "Lord's Army," as one children's song put it. They were on their way to the fire, the hassling, the invasive touches. If I wasn't careful, they'd take me with them. Even if I never got around to blaspheming the Holy Spirit, whatever that meant, they'd peer-pressure me into committing sins, forgivable but unconfessed. Then, a car would hit me. Or a witch, a real witch, would kill me. I wouldn't have time to make my apologies to God, so off to hell with me, my soul. Off to endlessly repeat the action that brought me there. The risk of moral contamination from my peers was too high. I'd reach through the risk, attempt friendship, but then feel afraid of what I'd done. I moved into myself, where I thought I heard God waiting, listening.

Though my church was consciously un-Freudian, it seemed to grasp that thinking about an action could connote a latent desire to take said action. The more fully Freudian subtleties—that such connections are nonlinear, temporally confused, spatially displaced—were swapped with pure Evangelical paranoia: if it's a thought about a sin, it's a sinful thought. Thinking about blasphemy of the Holy Spirit indicated that I wanted to commit the act. God already knew I had this want. He waited for me to give him a reason to leave. He dared me to step out my door while the angel of death passed. He'd never see me again. No one would. Nothing to see. It's unbearable to be without an image of oneself, "image" being a very poor word for countless encounters with oneself. This image might well be made through touch or sound, through an object that makes for a strange sadness. It's pleasure to spread even a very poor image of yourself. But a Christian's image is not what he senses of himself. The Christian's self-portrait delineates what God knows about him. My Christian image was a capture of this taboo thought, thought of as desire.

If God knew about my inner putrefaction, then Holly probably knew. Probably the pastor too. God had even told the heathen government. On the edge of a gray cubicle, I sat in the Westmoreland County Assistance Office while my mother completed welfare paperwork. My older siblings contributed to rent as they could, and some church members gifted us boxes of discount groceries, but there were still budgetary and dietary gaps. Welfare, which my extended family loudly denounced as a handout for the wimpy and weak-willed, had become necessary. Bored, and perhaps sensing my mother's shame, I interrupted her form-filling with questions and complaints. She tried to occupy me with Life Savers candy and random junk in her purse.

I looked toward the welfare-office worker. The worker avoided my gaze, obviously trying not to give me any sort of attention.

"Do you want to have food to eat?" My mother, in her idiosyncratic way, was trying to impress upon me the importance of all the ink going onto paper and all the concentration she needed to make the marks.

The welfare worker's avoidant eyes posed other questions: What was so wrong with looking at me? Was I even there? (Paperwork filed, documentation requested, decision pending.) After the ink was dry, and my mother's pride diminished, we waited for Holly's minivan to take us back home. Winter bluster cut through my coat, and various digits lost touch with the rest of me.

If I let you peer into the fluorescent-lit office where I waited, please don't mistake the hunger in my little stomach for the real suffering. The stomach is the easiest organ to fill. The real suffering is the failure to complete a form.

More than the loss of a singular connection, no matter how great, hell came to symbolize a widening disconnect from all creation—forever a ghost queuing outside a cubicle in an empty government building, each word in thought going unheard. Even the God who dared me to jump is gone. The death I was taught to fear, the death I began living, was one wherein I no longer have a reflection, no longer materialize beyond flashes of a broken subjectivity that claims the perspective of an *I* but can never confirm a *you* or *it,* and yet cannot stop the shearing pulse of *I,* like reaching out to touch you and then my hand slips through and flies away and won't come back. You look at me as though nothing has happened. Nothing to see.

Empty stares were the promise of Y2K. Before design gave our devices human voices, filled our screens with friendly faces, computers—to me—felt cold. Perhaps it was the unfamiliar green glow of a terminal or the rigid syntax of computer languages. Computers couldn't guess what I meant, wouldn't wade into my words to find what's under the water. The blank, incurious countenance of the early PC had a mirror in the faces of "secular" people. People outside my church were pejoratively labeled this way. "Secular" implied hollowness, depravity, and bile. The secular world wanted to abort every Christian baby, molest those of us who made it to birth. These monsters had no capacity to look in another's eyes and feel. They were locked in themselves—my nightmare—and they loved it. It was the secular world that would invade our house after the Y2K bug ended law and order, that would eat the flesh from my living bones, their stomachs acidic altars to Satan.

The biting mouths, the empty eyes, the gripping hands didn't arrive from outside. Five, ten, twenty, forty-six minutes after midnight on January 1, 2000, and nothing chilling was headed toward our house other than the howl of dogs frightened by fireworks. My mother never came down the stairs. The tears dried on my face. Everyone around me had spoken so seriously about the computerized doom-to-come. Some discussed burying food in trenches or buying even more guns. Nobody did any of it. I cried in my basement alone, having nothing to see. Of all the messages God could have sent, he never told me the Y2K panic was a scam. He watched me fall for it.

I never knew when God might let me embarrass myself this way. The same churchwomen who'd laid hands on my back cast and prayed for a miraculous recovery reconvened one Thursday morning in the church sanctuary to treat my spiritual maladies. The account of my contemporary sins is lost to me, but Holly felt that all my sinning was due to a demonic presence lodged inside my body. I wasn't allowed to leave the room until the women's regiment dealt with the intruder. In their weekday best, they surrounded me with a circle of joined hands. I was inflamed: eyes burning and puffy, face cooking in the heat of embarrassment. I'd begged them not to do this, refused to move from my pew chair for several minutes. The word "exorcism" might bring to mind theatrical, supernatural scenes: stodgy enrobed officials barking Latin at foamy children who are tied to their chintz beds. Protestants move the melodrama from scene to psyche. Encircling me, the adults of my everyday life shouted at me—in

English and otherworldly tongues—and demanded I change. Supposedly, they were speaking to the demon they'd discovered, but I couldn't corroborate their suspicions. The demon within was missing. I looked, I checked, and I could only find myself in there. Me, my sin, and a god waiting for a ride. They cast out my human needs, told my child desires to get gone. Sobbing, losing the rhythm of my breath, and then

I forget. It's frustrating to some people that I forget. I'm grateful for lapses in memory. I remember enough, and I distrust the desire of some to have a whole story. The story-wanters believe that, secretly, I'm hiding a powerful truth inside me, if only I'd find it while they shout. No demons were cast out in that sanctuary though. There are no demons and no hope of escaping them to be found inside me. There's me, a heavy dead God, and the memory of a sin he wanted me to commit.

God wasn't alone in wanting sin from me. As a tradition, my mother's stepfather would craft wooden paddles in his molding basement—somewhere in the area of canned tomatoes and a vice grip used to crack walnuts. Nobody ever ate the tomatoes. They were grown and canned as the Depression Era compulsion of two locals who had subsisted on farming and, in rough times, bartending. Fresher cans from the store outshone the dusty homemade jars, but the jars had a depth of light. You could see through them, maybe to the back of the shelf, to something empty. The paddles were birthday presents for his grandchildren. Mine, true to his style, had my name scrawled across it in Sharpie.

I don't remember going into the basement until after the stroke that left my grandfather unable to use his underground workshop. He must've had the stroke when I was three or four years old. My relatives said that, during the vascular event itself, he became enraged and fought my uncle in the yard. I think guns were involved. There must've been other symptoms, too, since that would've hardly registered as unusual. He was a man of grinding anger and one and one-third lungs; he was wounded in the Pacific theater of World War II. A writerly cliché would continue on: in place of the lung grew an intense anti-Asian hatred. I'm sure that hatred was in his bones before he left the American shore though. He hated everyone who wasn't white and even some white people. He held grudges from childhood and shouted blubbery blue streaks of jowls and toothless gaps from his wheelchair. From the stories his children told, he was an inconsiderate and vindictive father.

It scares me to think what must've agitated inside his mind once his body would no longer enact his rages. What depths of Oedipal fury were inside him, him sleeping downstairs and cared for like a child by his wife, his wife who slept upstairs? I don't know if my grandmother was relieved or saddened by the ceiling/floor that separated their nights. I know she didn't seem to try to resent the stairs.

Some prophecy must've come his way, warned him that one day his legs would no longer carry his hands down the wood-paneled hallways to beat children. Those decades would end. So he made himself into paddles. Mine was some kind of dark lacquered-plywood machination. The flat handle was roughly one-third of the total width. A sort of poor calligraphy carried out the words "Danny's Saddle Paddle." I remember it hitting my ass, clothed and not. I remember it cracking against my knuckles. My parents or grandparents moved the paddle by the handle, but its real movement came from me—carrying my own name inward as a punishment. I learned I could beat myself if no one else was around. If God was too busy, I could always strike myself dead. I could worry myself to hell while he waited and watched.

When virus arrived, when I started waiting on my sofa, God began watching me again. I was living next to the *Opuntia* cactuses that are always copying their images across the desert. *Opuntia*'s reduplicated ovals are called "paddles," but they're without handles. To grip it, you put your hand on the living thing coated in thorns that, depending on the species, may be small and meant to break off under the skin or may extend an inch or more out from the green surface, with honesty. Tucsonans grow *Opuntia* as fences, like we of the clay dirt grow yew or arborvitae. Maybe you'll push through a stand of evergreen fencing with a few scrapes to show, but finding your way through an *Opuntia* fence is nonsense. The thick thumps of green don't move much. As many plants do, the *Opuntia* grow in geometric arrangements meant to capture all the incoming sunlight. No room for leggy humans going the wrong way amid their paddles.

To walk through *Opuntia*, you have to lie to yourself. You have to believe you're a mind more than a body. You have to commit to not needing solace or comfort, safety or pause. You have to hold in the pain, rack up the thorns. You have to be good and disappear. Nothing to see. You have to want to become eternal. You have to hold your breath. You have to have a good reason. To walk through the *Opuntia*, you have to commit the unforgivable against yourself, keep a dead god alive, and he's all you ever see. Nothing to see.

I left my living room, undusted, in the early days of the pandemic, and I tried not to breathe. We were all trying not to breathe, except the ones who truly couldn't. During the day, the rays of the thirsty sun unceasingly crush space between star and *Opuntia* and generate a fricative sound, a hissing of the desert. *Opuntia*'s stomata—the microscopic pores along its paddles—are closed during the day, part of its photosynthesis routine called CAM, or Crassulacean acid metabolism.

In other styles of photosynthesis, plants exude wastewater from their stomata as part of daytime respiration. Desert plants using CAM have adapted to conserve water by keeping their stomata closed during the day, denying the sun its sacrifice. An evolutionary accomplishment, this mechanism allows *Opuntia* to flourish in intense desert heat where broad-leaved plants desiccate to gray-brown shadows. When the sun abates, *Opuntia* opens its stomata. Night fills with the remainders of life's most fundamental processes, and the moon streaks shadows behind shapes of excess. Night is made for *Opuntia*: a time of openness.

At night, I caught up with the long breaths I'd ignored during the day. If I prayed at night, I prayed to forget night and get back to day as quickly as I could, get back to holding my breath. In the early days, I ran through all the risks of grocery shopping, of touching shopping cart handles, of hearing someone cough. I felt good and I was lucky. Then, I waited again. My clock was the *Opuntia*. At night, our toxins flowed out. *Opuntia*'s met the air; mine stayed close, seeped back into my pores.

I'm not an *Opuntia*. I told you we don't have roots, and now I have to tell you we're not cactuses. We're misrecognition on a pulse, seeing ourselves everywhere all wrong. A bad image is much better than no image, however. No image is an impossible loneliness.

Come out in the sun with me and sweat and breathe, and we won't be cactuses anymore. We won't be plants, we won't have roots. We'll be bad images burning up, alive, opening outward. We'll be something to see.

Seaweeds, If You Can Believe It

When you hear the ocean, who comes to mind?

I think of Marta, my phonetics professor, who told me these are high-frequency fricative sounds I'm hearing. Incalculable aqueous waves collapsing into one another and pushing air particles aside. Complex, tightly spaced sinusoidal forms of noise are cramming their way to the front, to the beach, to my ears, and I'm forgetting where I am.

Relief.

A Carnival Cruise ship in the distance crowds up with passengers who are living loudspeakers, concentrating slowly toward dining rooms and auditoriums. If someone shouts "Mary!" in the dining room, how many people hear the call, and how many turn? The sounds shake many ears, but how many hum like a tuning fork? How many are Mary?

Water flops onto my feet and swiftly deposits a mess of seaweed. You could be forgiven for thinking seaweeds are plants, but only some of them are. "Seaweed" is an imprecise term, referring to multiple phyletic groups of algae without a common ancestor: red, brown, and green.

Green algae photosynthesize and are thus in the taxonomical kingdom *Plantae* with roses and pine cones; red and brown algae float in other directions. Blue-green algae are sometimes referred to as "seaweed," though they are in fact a bacterial life form rather than an algal. Neither weed nor algae; just blue-green. Botanists believe today's land plants emerged from the seas as a variation on green algae, and now I am staring down at my feet and ankles, which emerge from a secondhand lavenderish synthetic ladies' leisure suit that bears the label "California Wear."

I am in California, but the wrong California for this outfit. This outfit was to be worn on the back patio of the 1970s, surrounded by elephant ear and philodendron, resting on a whitewashed wicker loveseat, and being interviewed by Barbara Walters. She will ask me what I am going to do with my retirement or about the days of the studio system. I'm still smoking because it's still fashionable. I will give this outfit away to a charity shop in three years. The outfit will wind its way to Tucson, Arizona, and be worn, decades later, by some kind of perfumed crisis on a beach. The liquids on the surface of the seaweed move so quickly that they seem to shimmer, blinding me from alternate vantage points so I can never get a visual fix on its texture or dimensions.

Flop.

More water carries away the mass. My feet miss the sensation and my eyes are strained from trying to sense.

I don't know when I was first called a faggot but I think it was kindergarten. A child with no homosexual knowledge threw the term at me but it didn't hurt because I didn't know what a faggot was, and I was too busy being curious about the word "faggot" to care about the derision he intended, or his sneer, or how he was right. Other kids picked up on the word and used it as an informal address. Something about it stuck. My wobbly wrists, jutting hips, rolling eyes, flowery run all served as resonating chambers, and somehow "faggot" had the right frequency to be amplified by my body and mind. I was undeniably a faggot, shaped by the cosmos to do faggotry, cavities of my body clamoring with exuberant fagfulness. I wonder where that kid learned the word—had he been called a faggot too? Was his father caught sucking dick, leading his mother to shout, "You fucking faggot!" Was it said about a distant relative? A grocery shop cashier? Elton John on television? Who was calling out, "Mary!" and why?

Adults explained "faggot" to me with an unexplanation.

"It's a bad word, don't use it."

"Fuck" was also explained this way, along with the middle finger. In fact, the middle finger was defined as the visual equivalent of "fuck." The middle finger means fuck which means something you can't say but which is the middle finger. Here were two symbols locked in a circuit, meaning nothing except the other one. Because of its irreducible nature, I misunderstood the middle finger to be erotic for a while. I felt a precocious flush when I saw a man giving another man the middle finger on television, blithely unaware of the secondary meanings of my own arousal and the world of men giving men fingers on- and off-screen.

"Faggot" didn't seem erotic in the same way because, unlike "fuck" and the center digit, "faggot" was about me specifically. "Fuck" was a gambit or provocation. "Faggot" was a taxonomical position, a scientifically determined piece of information about me, a reading of outward signs to determine true inner identity. There was nothing more to be said that anyone could bear to say. To name me was to name a sin, and my own name implied my wretchedness. Snot and tears and gastric juices would churn up as my paranoia turned accuser, prosecutor, judge, and reclaiming devil. To be more like God, I became his insecure omniscience and most unmerciful contours. Of course, I was a faggot.

The "g" of "faggot" next to the schwa sound comes from throaty shadows. The pure and holy vomit at the truth revealed by calling me a faggot. A beached whale disgorging its meal of not-yet-dead creatures. Oh God, the faggot lives.

Memories from inside the gut are hard to come by.

Jess said, "You know, right?"

And I said, "What?"

And she said, "That you're gay."

And then I was gay.

A newly oriented college freshman, "gay" was another draping of independence wrapped around me. I had a dorm room, to which I came and from which I left as I pleased. I had a schedule full of classes I'd chosen and rarely attended. I had very little cash, but I spent it as I wished. Tying it all together, a miniature T-shirt stretched across my torso that wordlessly pronounced,

I'm gay now, and you will address me as such!

"Gay" is monosyllabic, starting at the back of the throat and moving to the hard palate and trailing off like a forceful declaration of who you are, followed by a gentle reminder that you don't want to rock the boat or upset anyone and so we don't have to talk about this anymore if you don't want to I just thought it was important to say so . . .

"Faggot" ends with [t], a dental stop. Full stop on the bones cracking space between them. Cockbiter. Or perhaps it ends with a glottal stop, a closing of the back of the throat, a damming up of what the speaker feels spurting upward. "Gay" has different waveforms and does not resonate the same as "faggot." When gay fell into my freshman body in the warm Pittsburgh fall of 2004, it resonated with a certain refinement of shopping-mall style, a certain Applebee's decorum, a certain je ne sais quoi, which means it really wasn't certain because *si tu ne sais quoi*, then it's not possible to be certain, *tu comprends?* Gay *c'est gai—c'est français.*

Gay was like a library card for gay knowledge, or maybe a Google search history transmuted into an Amazon "Products You Might Like" list. Gay was meeting men on Gay.com, hoping my shoes were sexy enough, being impressed by a hot tub, never liking anything, claiming to hate women for no apparent reason—*toujours gai, toujours gai comme Eartha dit.* Gay was taking up my cross as the most maligned, the "new Black," the patron saint of unending discrimination who means no harm, my dear, it's just a joke.

I learned my divas, learned my words, learned how a gay bar works and how to get a drink and how not to get a date, and I learned that it was OK to care how I look. Beauty is not capitulation; asceticism is not victory. I now knew that Dan Savage was not a WWF wrestler, and condoms came in an array of flavors that all tasted like flavored condom. Gay was faggot in a suit, maybe. Or faggot in True Religion jeans on the eve of 2007, up in the gym, just working on *his* fitness. There is something consistent in gay, or rather something with the appearance of consistency. Gay moves with the trends wherever they come from, those odd waves, and can be traced. Gay is a résumé with no unexplained gaps in employment but a blackout or two on weekday nights. Gay is watching *Will & Grace*. Faggot is Eric McCormack—*no, no*—Sean Hayes shoving a toothbrush up his asshole to touch his prostate two hours before bedtime. Faggot is always vomiting up something uncouth and sloppy because that [g] sound won't go away, won't stop churning up the "gut" of the "fag-gut."

And what business of it is yours, Blake? I never asked you to use my toothbrush! You borrowed it. You knew what kind of faggot I am.

I wasn't good at gay in the way that I'm very good at faggot. I was too manic, too difficult. No proper character development, no progress, no glint of a helpful disposition. I still refuse to have a wedding episode, a peaceful cast reunion. And look at all the stories I still refuse to tell, the memories I can't be bothered to cobble together. Utterly useless to the liberation front. Alexis Carrington-Colby from *Dynasty*: sharp, impossible, unwilling to wait for the other guests to be seated before devouring life. Eventually, I backed away from gay, or it backed away from me (gay is too polite to tell me), and it ran back out into the coursing depths. But I'm thankful to gay. I was gay in between turns of being a faggot. I'm still a little gay. If you don't know what that means, I can't help you. You're probably straight and not even God can help you.

Does it make you angrier to see yourself clearly and not love what you see, or to see yourself distorted and to be told it's really you? I'm asking because I've seen so many reflections as the waves come in—my head fractured and sutured by/with bubbles, chin drawn down into the earth's core where magma does electrolysis, mouth dissolved. I once stared into a puddle in my driveway until I believed it was a portal into another world, until I believed what I saw were trees in another universe and not a reflection of the tree twenty feet from my house. I am looking into the ocean waves, and they keep insisting back with pictures they say are of me, but I'm trying to see the sand below the wave. Optics are tricky. I am in my own way again, both meanings.

Not long after I became gay, a quartet of local transsexuals and cross-dressers came to my university for a public-awareness event. (Those, I know, are not the of-this-moment terms, formed into fine sans serif fonts, forwarded by trans advocacy groups. Not every wave on the shore now was on the shore moments ago.) Mostly middle-aged, mostly white, these girls were part of a decades-old network of people *like that* who socialized in gay bars, hotel conference rooms, private homes, and the ladies' section of Kaufmann's Department Store. Some of them loved drag queens and the nightlife. Others were reserved professionals, anxious not to be mixed up with lowbrow theater. They spoke carefully and sagely, in the way any grown-up sounds sage and careful to an eighteen-year-old. They talked about sex and its double meanings. Other students in the room chuckled softly at the tension between what they *thought* a woman looked like and the looking like these women were doing. Some listened sincerely, like the admitted students they were. I, me, I was lost to all my peers, eyes full of cold sparkle and asking to be pierced through

Look at me so I know I can be seen.

Those visitors could have asked me to get back in Holly's van, and I would've already been fastening my seatbelt.

Don't you know you're still alive and full of what you haven't yet been? And aren't you, yes, I mean, you, hands all over my words, holding me like you hold a face, I mean you, aren't you dying to flash out through all those possibilities, like a dying light bulb burning up for no reason except that it can?

Around that same time, my friend John and I began performing in drag. We sparked and sputtered at local bars and then, when local bars wouldn't have us, performed on city streets.

Veronica, né John, was all synthetic blond hair tangled into the chaos of a rocker-chick-pop-camp-Jodie-Garland-Christmas-garland-and-what-have-you-come-as? aesthetic. Something for everyone. My own early performances were angry and a touch on the nose: knives hacking at cucumbers, sacred texts ripped apart, baby dolls burned with cigarettes on Christmas Eve. Nothing for no one. My makeup name was "Lilith," but stylized to DanieLilith on internet platforms. A few years later and I was performing as "Daniel," but with the etymological tribute to God, *-el*, cut off. Dani and Lamorte, maudlin and reactive. I was an out-of-work demon and an unconvincing vixen; an unscheduled, knock-kneed pop tribute and a caterwauling mytho-psycho-retro hag. I floated through circuits of sincere artifice and cumbersome certainty, fag-this, trans-that. I saw those guest speakers around town, shyly learned their names again, let them look at me and tell me what I looked like. In the mirror and camera, I made new images of myself. I glimpsed myself, as a kind of guest speaker, a kind of event, a kind of explaining the chuckles and sympathies in the room.

At a critical point in all this floating, my day job was to answer, forward, or delete emails about stained dresses—customer service at an internet retail start-up. The owner's dog shit on the floor and an open bottle of tequila atop the break-room refrigerator came in lieu of pay raises. It was 2009. Bubbles were bursting, friends were graduating into joblessness. I'd dropped out years before, found work somehow. Without the abysmal economic situation, someone might have noticed I was habitually late to every job I had, half-asleep more than half my shift. All that childhood insomnia caught up with me. The slightest implication that I was trapped, by a desk or a routine, and I was on the edge of losing consciousness.

The dog-shit job gave me a discount on company goods, which were almost exclusively garments for twentysomething women and we who pretend to still be something like that. Frugality was my first excuse for all the frocks on my body.

I mean, at this price, I might as well wear it.

My coworkers were largely supportive of my digressions, especially Maggie. She and I bonded over a shared inability to let go of a good joke, even if it meant making the whole company our punch line. Maggie was, let's just say, head writer for the company website. I don't know if that's true, but I owe her, so let's go with it: "head writer." Her copy tended toward anti-sales, full of puns and references that treated the reader to the joy of ideas, not the joy of imagining oneself in a cheap pinup swimsuit that fades in the wash.

"This is one swimsuit you can't wear to the Second Wave."

"Sometimes it's sexy to look like you can't have your own credit card!"

She didn't write any of that, but I'd like to think she would. We weren't the same but we weren't wholly different.

The bar formed a tertiary point in my workaday transit: home, work, bar. Again and again. Drag and fag makes sense in bars. Bars remind you that there are things to numb, reasons to go senseless. I'd stand senseless along a wall or a bit of dance floor when a man would approach, seemingly out of nowhere. Plaid button-down curving over a belly, and glasses that say "job foreman" or "accounts manager." He'd offer to buy me breast implants and make me his (certainly secret) girl. There wasn't any conversation leading up to the offer. He didn't even know my name

or, wait, no, I've probably got that wrong.

He almost certainly had a wife somewhere, maybe multiple, and other somewhat secret girls. From work, he'd driven five or six miles out of his way, winding a confused path to the gay bar. Cold War spies would do the same, trying to lose surveillance agents on their tails. Nobody would ever know he was here. There'd be no reports. He paid in cash, only spoke to the bartender in an abbreviated lexicon. "Coor's." "Iron City." "Budweiser." I never quite wanted breasts, but his offer wasn't off the mark. I wanted *something* to change, and in every way, I could not afford it. To his disappointment, my wants didn't include being hidden away. I declined, wouldn't let him rescue me from flatchestedness.

For many years, I was a faggot in my ecology of t-girls, chasers, unsteady drag queens, and cross-dressers in dusky dive bars. We weren't quite the same, but we weren't wholly different, and often we were same and different at once, and then none at all. We came together and drifted apart because we were desirous of one another's fantasies, and exchanging fantasy for fact was simply no fun. Our spaces were crowded.

Do letters in bottles really wash up on shores? I've never seen it. I stand and wade and splash and look and the letter never gets there, and I wonder if it's even been sent. Let's put an island right in the middle of all the oceans, and I'll go live there with bottles of paper. Sometimes I find an address on the map and write a postcard to someone I do not know. I write them words I do not understand. I do not include a return address.

Niches narrow. Bowl cuts and blunt bangs brought taxonomical news: scientists had split the desire atom. Now, sexuality and gender were two distinct entities. The break had been achieved before, several times, in several decades, but now the general public was getting a glimpse at a space held in between. Like the earth revolving around the sun, or the number of licks it takes to get to the center of a Tootsie Pop, empirical study had gifted us a new truth. When it came to describing me, "gay" and "faggot" were outmoded, behind the times. I'd been misdiagnosed at birth, but perhaps it wasn't too late to save me. My transition began. Not a transition in the accepted sense but in the more generic sense of something moving from one theme to another, from one frame to another. Within the zeitgeist of transgender academia, "trans" is beloved for its meaning of "across." Now, non-binary was washing across me, my eyes moving across it. Never mistake eyes for passive organs.

A local gay rag confirmed the news by nominating me for a "voice of the non-binary" award. Never mind that I hadn't taken up the moniker myself just yet. Taxonomical identification requires two who speak on uneven terms. There was an awards ceremony in a bar basement, but all memory of that has left me. I was likely drunk, which is a great way to be when everyone's staring at you, calling you a name that isn't yours, that has no resonance inside of you. Still, there was flash and sparkle to this new word, "non-binary." It carried the cheapest of dreams: the dream of matching. I wasn't wholly different from, but not completely the same as, those guest speakers, those breast-offering men, Maggie and the dog-shit clothes, Veronica and John and the people who watched us. But sometimes, when courage wanes, and in isolation, I hear my own wish to just be the same, to do away with the messy tension of being similar but not same. "Non-binary" seemed, to me, at first, undefined enough that I'd finally relax in my own matching. Eventually, though, faggots return to the antagonisms which pump the blood in our veins. It's not that we *aren't* men, it's that we aren't any good at it. Or anything, really. We are useless to the bank account, the community garden, and the co-op. In that uselessness, though, we glimpse something before the next wave draws our attention elsewhere. Sometimes our memory of that glimpse fades, and we wonder if we should just sit back in our wicker furniture and answer questions. We can't. We're not very good at sitting still.

No science evades skeptics. In another bar, forgetting another thing, I found myself talking to another local performer. Scattered among the drinkable inventory, and along the cash registers, were cheap hats. They'd been hot glued into misery, with shiny red feathers and bits of mesh that no self-respecting orange would ever wear.

Imagine if there were a band called Panic! at the Haberdashers. Something like that.

My drinking companion had made them, begun hawking them at the bar for extra cash. She worked for her family, and they seemed to pay her whether she worked or not. All her family worked for her family. That sort of family. The hats were that sort of craft. Our conversation was a discharge of lines mostly meant for the speaker to hear. Then, suddenly, I had her attention. I'd called myself non-binary, wondered if I might be something else, too, a *trans-y something.*

"No" was her response, laughing, disbelieving, like I'd said I thought I might actually be from the lost continent of Atlantis.

I tried again, and, again, she pressed back. She did not see the evidence. Whatever it was she saw, surely it was simply fag.

I was a poor fit for non-binary, anyhow. I've never been predisposed to openness, to softness, to infusing each moment with mindfulness and meaningfulness. And I resent astrology, the non-binary science. I won't have "up there" up my there again. I'm still too loud, still trying to take over the Carrington Atlantic Oil Company and kick that bitch Krystle out of my mansion. I'm all camp in luxurious furs, and if fur is murder, then let us murder the world!

If this account seems too far-fetched, if I am unable to know precisely where the lines of doing and done-to lie, just recall watching a movie in a theater and going places without moving your body. Our insistence that one's difference must be contained in words makes it hard to admit how much of knowing oneself is ignorance of ignorance. What I know myself to be is that for which I do not yet have evidence to the contrary. I was a fag, who had been gay, who was tested for non-binary, but that's about all I knew.

If there are true positives and false positives, and true negatives and false negatives, can there be true transsexuals and false transsexuals? That is to say, can one be neither trans nor cis, since a false positive is neither a true positive nor a true negative? I am losing my sense of whether this is a we or a they, a me or a you. Am I a false transsexual? The term almost sounds redundant. What I'm talking about is someone—and maybe I'm that someone—who *seems* trans but just isn't quite. Nothing's right, but things aren't quite wrong in the right way. These are difficult questions to follow, I think, because we've worn such deep tracks into these paths: trying to name ourselves, trying to survive knowledge of our difference, trying to throw murderous sects off the scent. Trans people are always suspected of being false—a cowardly panic. A false trans person is a trans person who proves the stereotype true even though the stereotype is false. Appearances are deceiving. Proving the stereotype right is a resonance cavern in the body of the faggot. We are that of which gay shame is made—errant outliers, cyanobacteria and seaweeds messing up the clean lines of taxonomy.

I duck to avoid a seagull flying too low and lose sight of my body, eyes closing and I crumple up.

Transgender happened to me like a transition—in parts, slowly, levels of proximity and distance ever-shifting. I don't really know the day I started using "transgender" to describe myself, unlike "gay" which comes with a very gay anecdote. Waves crested, crashed, retreated, and then there I was in 2016 with a transgender job and transgender words. I had been hired as a temporary office worker for a transgender studies center at a university in Tucson. It was a scandal. The hiring committee originally selected a recent-released gender and women's studies PhD and sent me a very nice "thanks, but no thanks" email. We called the GWS building "the women's prison," owing to its compound-like architecture and vicious infighting among the faculty housed there. That I remain a dedicated feminist after so many encounters with that department is a testament to the sincerity of my politics. The new doctor was adequate on the job, but she was, she admitted, not trans of any sort. Some of the trans graduate students and faculty were frustrated by her appointment and grumbled on my behalf. The grumbles proved useful when the good doctor was poached by a dean of who knows what, just three months into the job, leaving a new old vacancy.

For my first day as the second choice, I selected a skirt of gem-tone blues, greens, and purples and a neutral top. My long curls pulled back, my lips lost under a slab of matte fuchsia lipstick, I pedaled my bike toward campus in the July sun. I was now like those women I'd seen in downtown Pittsburgh, wearing silken formal separates with sneakers. They walked from the law office to a lunch at the hotel with their pumps in a bag. Locking up my bike, I slipped out of my biking shoes and into bold red heels with a silver stripe along the edge. This is probably one of the most powerful transformations a person can undertake.

My office was located in a former sorority dormitory at the quiet eastern edge of campus. Almost no one worked in the building, but the women's room, officially gender-neutral, had at least ten toilets. Next to the sinks, a door led to unlit shower stalls where, almost certainly, horror film goblins hid. In late summer, the inside and outside of the building were equally abandoned. Students wouldn't be seen for a few more weeks yet.

Searching through the onboarding emails on my phone, I found the building door code, punched it in, and went upstairs to find no one waiting for me. The business manager for our unit was out running errands, unaware that this day was my first. When she returned, breathless from the 110-degree heat, she sent me out to complete my new employee paces. I tried the day's look on administrators and laborers, who weren't even aware of anything transgender being studied nearby, as I collected an employee ID and tax forms, and scheduled new employee trainings. I was not trying to be a woman as much as I was simply trying to be something a university could bear to hire as a public face. I would have to visit the conservative hubs of campus: budget offices, deans' meeting rooms, any department that issues a door key or requires forms by fax. My attire needed to say: "I am a known thing, a professional and legally recognized thing."

A few weeks into the job, my unit came under the leadership of a new administrator: a short, gray-haired woman who dressed like she taught piano in the morning and then recited poetry to reluctant dinner guests at night. You know—the drapings. On her first day in the building, she stopped by my office door to introduce herself and welcome me as a fellow newcomer. I stood, unfolding my legs, to return the greetings, and saw her eyes widen as though I were pathogenic mud rising from a putrid ditch, taking on human form as a sort of mockery. I knew this look. It was the look construction workers gave me years earlier, when I sauntered toward my dog-shit workplace in a minitunic with tight leggings. They'd whistled from afar, but as my image resolved in the backs of their eyes, so, too, did their self-loathing for having wanted me or perhaps having wanted to be me. The line between the two is so thin. I imagine inside their eyes my image morphed into the sticky floor of a men's room, a wasted Band-Aid clinging to the edge of a dumpster—something to be cleansed with fire. Whatever attempts I had made at being a "known thing" had led me toward being known as a disease, disaster, or torment is known. Whatever I was, whatever I am, "transgender" was not an adequate warning label. The new boss and I shook hands and made small talk. Her wife was my professor. This had to go well. It didn't.

The beginning of the fall semester filled the campus with bodies enrolled and visiting. An international trans studies conference, organized by our center, brought people to Tucson from each continent, each with their own idea of what it is to travel across the boundaries of body and desire. The lead-up to the conference had been, in my own experience, an almost corporate slog of insufficient forms and gruff emails. Marketing for the conference positioned it as a first of its type, and everyone wanted a good look at themselves and "the field." At the registration table, people saw my name badge and recognized me from all those forms and emails. They greeted me, and I tried to look confident, like those guest speakers had looked confident when they surveyed the nervous, desirous freshman in the front row. I assuaged fears about overhead projectors, apologized for typos, and pointed to a map that showed attendees how to get from here to there without getting beat up along the way. As the first night's keynote speech began, and with everyone registered, the hall cleared, I stepped onto a small balcony. Without knowing, I began to sob. I sobbed in disbelief, not knowing which organ had produced these tears and how they could be mine.

Unlike faggot or gay, transgender has two instances of the letter "r," which, thanks to a childhood speech impediment, I could not pronounce at the time I was pronounced a faggot. My variety of American English bunches the tongue back toward the molars and closes the nasal passage to produce [ɹ], as in "ramrod." Instead of [ɹ], my childhood self produced [w], as in "wayward," lips pursed in a tight loop then stretched open to let air proceed in a shaft from the lungs. A few years of speech therapy taught me to curve my tongue backward in a collapsed orca fin and approximate [ɹ] enough to convince other American English speakers that I was using the correct sound.

I dreamed one night that I was writing my family name on a document. Suddenly, I realized I had been misspelling my name all my life, leaving out the "r" that in waking hours was never there. In the dream, I realized I had run, like the red robin and rouge roosters about which speech therapists asked me to speak, from the letter "r" in my own name so my name wouldn't be something only others could say. Another faggot fantasy: self-naming. How many faggots spent youthful hours concocting pseudonyms, noms de plume, for their endless fantasies? How many of us imagined all manner of bodies and bodily rapports before we quite knew what all those imaginations could mean? I love "faggot" because I can say all the sounds myself, even if they were a gift from elsewhere.

The day after the sobbing, I went to lunch with a trio of conference presenters, all young and ambitious. They came from New York, Los Angeles, and DC. They all talked about the smallness of Tucson, about their big grad student lives in big grad student cities. They talked, too, about things doctors might do for them or had already done for them. I followed along with the secondhand knowledge I'd acquired over time, but I had no experience to share. Whatever had led these three to work with and against medicine, I could not find the same desire inside myself. It's there but weak, or only visible from some angles. Maybe it's a shadow, an optical illusion, a leviathan in the river.

When I'm standing in the water, foam cutting me off at the knees, I'm not sunning myself on the sandy flats. When I'm being spun under waves, eyes clenched and laughs building up, I'm not walking parallel to the horizon in search of dewy purple shells. Soon, I'll shower and close off all these options for the day, but while the time is limited yet remaining, I try each motion on water and sand. Usually, I end up as deep as I can go, pouring out mouthfuls of seawater, hoping to lose contact with the floor. I'll never have much of a shell collection.

Away from the shore, dried and dressed, it's not so clear what I mean to do. A stream of semisincere wished lives flows through me, and while something appears steady at the center, I know it is only because some erosion is too slow to see. A boulder becomes sand in an amount of time that renders all names moot. There is no "real me" to get to, and so, when accused of not being a real woman, I do not feel outrage but instead relief. I could never figure out how to be a real man, how to want to be such a thing, and I have the whole of society encouraging me to sort it out. How could I hope to find a clear want to be a real woman, or a woman at all? When I call myself "transgender," I am confronted with the fact that I don't know which direction I mean to head in. Worse still, I get the sense that I want to move in all directions, all at once, and then change my mind, and then do it all over again. If a hallmark of being transgender is a persistent, legible want to find a steady form, even if that form is itself full of conflict, then maybe I've misrecognized myself in the term. Maybe, because no one noticed my mispronunciation, I forgot I was only approximating what everyone else was doing without actually doing it. Americans mistake hummingbird moths for hummingbirds while on vacation in Europe. The moths have long proboscises and beat their wings *fastfastfast*. But there are no true hummingbirds in Europe, only our hope to know one when we see one. That's not to say that I have escaped man or woman, that I have become a third leg adding new stability to an unsteady regime. Instead, I have come to think of myself as an insufficiency as these things are measured.

For very understandable reasons, "transgender" has undergone public relations revisions in recent decades. That's how I got that non-dog-shit job, after all. In the 1990s, people like Riki Wilchins, Kate Bornstein, and Susan Stryker wrote their way off the set of *Geraldo*, through the television screen, and into the theater, the city hall, the classroom. As long as trans people were a salacious mystery, they could not secure a right to stand in the waves, stare out to the horizon, forget their limits. They were viewed as contaminants, public health ailments to be institutionalized and dissected, or hints of a horizon researchers would never be brave enough to chase. But if it's proven in textbooks and court decisions that they're not tabloid riffraff, not a sign of worse things to come, then perhaps rights can be secured, limits forgotten. Now there are transgender studies journals, books, and centers. People whose politics are reminiscent of shower scum—harmless if unconsidered—put big signs in their yards: TRANS LIVES MATTER.

But here's the rub: I think all of us mixed-up this-thats—the fags and the homos and the butches and the pin-up lipsticks, the CDs and sissies and secret midnight plastic hair wearers, the old transsexuals and new transgender *people,* and even sometimes the loud-mouthed lady scorching her eyes on the horizon line—I think we're all still media junk and virulent spittle, to some. Some people really do loathe us, wish us fully dead, make it their life's mission to make our lives into missions, into projects of conversion and confession. If this is an unsteady position to find ourselves in, it's perhaps a boat we can rock at will.

Out of everyone, Myrna looked the most comfortable, in a literal sense, at my dog-shit job. She was immune to the overpriced buzz of fast fashion and kept a blanket draped across her lap at all times. Sometimes it crawled up, near her shoulders, her hands peeking out to do all the clicking and clacking that keeps an online store online. She became my supervisor once I finally took over customer service, after stints in warehouse and shipping. The CEO and owner of dog shit had done the old bait-and-switch on me: hired to send emails, then sent instead to ship packages. He did this a lot, maybe thought of it as saving up talent for a rainy day. He underestimated how annoyed and annoying I would be. I whinged and griped and sniped and snarled about my warehouse job to anyone who could potentially perceive the message in any sensory format. My complaints might've been quieter, had working conditions been better. While Mr. and Mrs. Dogshit toured Southern Europe, I stood, fully wrapped for winter, in an abandoned machine shop–turned-warehouse, pulling high-waisted, 1940s-style pants off a shelf. Chemical heat packs were jammed into every pocket, and I wove between space heaters on my way to the shipping station. Somewhere, a girl in Florida would wear these pants in a photo for one of the many social media platforms that would boom and bust. Right now, I couldn't feel my fingers. I had something like a cold, but who knows what it was. I was scheduled for *just* shy of forty hours, just shy of anyone being obligated to insure my health. Yes, I complained because the job was ugly, dirty, and uncelebrated. I also complained because I was cold and ill, and I deserved far better.

Now, seated next to Myrna and her blanket, I click-clacked emails to huffy teens and effusive fortysomethings who'd purchased their bit of retro-boho wearable miscellany. Myrna was like me, in the way that Maggie was like me, in the way that we weren't quite like each other, but none of us was quite right. My skirts and slapdash eye shadow weren't Myrna's style, but she appreciated not being seated next to a business school graduate.

Anything but that, surely.

When dog shit's shipping vendor came to discuss contract terms, the shipping company representatives asked to meet with me. I confessed to Myrna that I felt glum about the prospects of being treated intelligently, looking as I did, by people like shipping company representatives. The words are lost to me, but Myrna countered that if they thought me a freak, a faggot, a line of words used on *Sex and the City* but no longer uttered in polite conversation, that was a "them problem," not a "me problem." Even better, it might be a "me solution." I forget the words, but I got the gist.

I dressed recklessly for those meetings, like Tina Turner was going to Pee-wee's playhouse to give Phyllis Diller the Carol Channing Lifetime Achievement Award for Subdued Fashions and Demure Behavior (wink). In this new aesthetic schema, nothing could clash except for prudence. I dressed for the fantasy I wanted to live, left the practicalities of business to people with minds like staplers: one function, almost empty. I was here to take over the company.

Which company?! What a question!

For whatever reasons, some of us are more prone to seeing ourselves as problems. As a result, perhaps, we're quicker to understand when the social majority has come to agree: we are a problem. I don't think there's anything to be done about this assignation. Scapegoating is perhaps a perennial aspect of sociality. The best we can do is hope to miss our turn on the block and try to help others escape the pain. I'm no idealist.

"Transgender," like "non-binary" and "gay," contains a hope of getting it right. A hope for no longer being a problem. I know that, in more theoretical circles, and in youthful meme-laden enclaves, transgender life is treated as exploratory and experimental. I know, too, that there are limits to this. Very few people want their category of being interrogated at every turn, or want to live as nonentities in a legal landscape where being unnamed can only harm. Plenty of nonacademic trans people just want to get on with being a man or a woman, finally, in ways others can witness. It was this hopeful strain of transgender thought that caused me to see that this name, "transgender," couldn't do much for me. As it is configured for political talking heads and fundraising benefits, "transgender" is an adjective for the stable, for those with steady sight who see where they are and where they plan to go. Or at the very least, "here" and "there" undulate in harmony. "Transgender" has come to imply a stability I cannot find inside myself.

None of this is fixed. None of it should be fixed. There's nothing to fix, Mary. I could be transgender again, but we'd both have to change, OK? And anyway . . .

I am an old millworker's house in the Kiskiminetas Valley: foundations sagging and meltwater seeping in, front yard retaining walls giving way under neglect and dozens of winter freeze cycles, indoor plaster walls bulging apart, old mine runoff drizzling into the nearby crick and turning it the color of a creamsicle. I fill the gaps left open by mine subsidence, expand myself. I sometimes worry I will never be constrained, styled, contained, respectable, or reliable enough to merit proximity to others. I worry I will terminally out myself as a faggot, as something only to be named derisively, and all love given to me will be rescinded. You won't burn this book or give it away—you'll just abandon it to a place you never look. Have I already sinned too deeply? I take solace in being a faggot because you can never sin too deeply to be a faggot; a house can never be too ruined to be condemned. I want to see how far I can sink into the mud, to know the last moment before the walls give way. I want to live, not succeed.

In her 1987 classic "Incognito," Céline Dion sings something that, in English, might sound like "Incognito. I'm restarting my life at zero." She's getting away behind her oversized music video sunglasses, going to Florida maybe. From the reflective snows of Québec to the reflective oceanic sands of Admiral's Cove. Unknown and starting at zero. Not a one or a two but a not a knot a naught a gnaught which is not a word. Not gay, not transsexual, not transgender, just an unknown faggot. Céline tells us she's going far from here / from you / from herself, that she'll even forget her own name. But was it her name to begin with? Maybe Céline's body hums at other names: Diane?

As taxonomic assignations wash away, I feel my body which is me relax. It is a delicious extension of living when people retool their bodies toward their fleshy dreams and when they insist on being known by names that refuse all heuristics. Blessed are those whose dreams can respond to the language of open eyes. Appetites pull in so many directions. Swim back out.

I grew up so far from the ocean that the sight of it still fills me with overwhelming joy. I didn't see the ocean until I was twenty-three. It's still new to me. The waves keep bringing me things I haven't seen before, and, even if they're not for me, I'm still grateful. I still open my eyes to let the light and seaweed overrun me.

Plant Fakes

You see it and you lose track of where you're going. Some trinket in a supermarket exit. Supermarket exits are meant to provoke a shopper's roundabout, drawing you back again to the cash register. Loop on loop until the exit of exhausted feet or exhausted wallet opens up. The enticement isn't always felt immediately, and many of us stream out the door not knowing that, one way or another, we're only widening the orbit.

Heading toward the "OUT" doors of a Safeway supermarket in Tempe, I slowed and paused near the floral display, eyes locked on bundles of Gerbera daisies shrieking their color out of a stout black bucket: a Starburst package of bright pink, sharp green, dreamy yellow. Each flower was stained a single color. Glitter glue slogged along the length of individual rays like television static. Bouquets of daisies, on conspicuously unadulterated green stems, were wrapped in that shining clear plastic that's audible to the eyes. Floral delicacy and stylistic impertinence were pressed so close, too close to keep myself from laughing, then gasping, then laughing, then more gasping. The flowers didn't look ridiculous themselves as much as they made the rest of the world seem stuck-up, fuddy-duddy. How can I take this world seriously when these are among its contents? I reached for my phone and took a few quick pictures to help me remember the daisies, but there was no chance I would ever forget them. I'm always circling back to them.

When I moved to Arizona, I had no particular interest in plants. My rural nooks of southwestern Pennsylvania were packed tight with black walnut and tumbles of goldenrod. A family interest in harvesting chestnuts and growing tomatoes meant I was never entirely ignorant of plants, but they formed a living surface for an unthought sense of home. I recognized local plants like I recognized the people who shivered alongside me waiting for the 8:32 a.m. bus in January, or the cashiers at the nearby supermarket. A face. Maybe a name. Little else known. Tucson, held low by the outspread fingers of rocketing palms and velveted with tender mesquite leaflets, was a total break in this lifelong pattern of ambiguously Appalachian foliage. Tucson plant life held poses and sharp lines that I found fascinating if also terrifying. Four-inch-long spines off a saguaro cactus or furious blooms on an ocotillo were inexplicable, and it was the lack of an explanation that led me back to plants again and again. A love of plants developed in me, developed me, planted me.

Start at the false top of a pineapple. *Cryptanthus* is a low-growing member of the botanical family *Bromeliaceae*, the genre of plants to which pineapple belongs. In fact, *Cryptanthus* looks like a pineapple top that has been pushed short and wide. Their wiggly, tapered leaves with sawtooth edges are striped with dark and light greens. If kept in bright light, the greens transform into pinks and maroons. The scientific name for the plant comes from the Latin bits "crypt" (hidden) and "anthus" (flower), because the flower at the top of the plant is hardly noticeable. On my own *Cryptanthus*, the spent flowers look like a left-behind pyramid of Shredded Wheat cereal. I purchased it sometime between arriving in Tucson and becoming something you can only praise: a community college librarian. I didn't mean to be a librarian. "Librarian" was the first job available en route to the job I wanted: "archivist." I wasn't a very good librarian, but I was bad enough that people mistook what I was doing for "innovation."

I kept a *Cryptanthus* on my office desk, planted in a small plastic pot, tucked inside a black ceramic calavera cache pot. The stiff, waxy leaves gave the skull a sort of hat and started conversations with students and professors who stopped by. I would nestle a selection of objects from my office in the hollows of my arms, carry them to the classroom, and ask students to describe them, dream up stories about them, fabricate connections between them: old photos, scraps of fabric, glass brooches. Then we would research to fill out those stories and test those connections. It was a way of playacting research and living real life. Among these objects was the *Cryptanthus* in its plastic pot. Students were regularly split on how to describe *Cryptanthus*. Some described the plant as "fake" or "plastic," while others were convinced it was "real." Each time the debate emerged, I listened silently for a minute as arguments were exchanged:

"It has dirt and roots, so it's real."

"The roots could be plastic. The dirt could be fake!"

The latter argument had its evidence positioned around the library: "fake" ornamental trees with polyester leaves flocked in thin dust. Planted in little baskets, the trees' molded-plastic roots were topped with a layer of possibly real moss-as-mulch and some kind of textured layer meant to approximate the soil line. With its waxy, thin leaves and its rigid structure, *Cryptanthus* appeared (to my students, anyway) to be more closely related to the plastic trees outside the classroom door than to anything else. The dry soil surrounding *Cryptanthus*'s roots was taken as additional evidence: Why wasn't the soil moist? Wouldn't I water it if it were real? Don't plants need a lot of water? Having cared for the plant myself, I was startled by how quickly students believed it was fake.

Sharp, weird, ugly, languishing in a library office, fine. OK, yeah, sure, but fake?

Fake ranges in meaning, from fake breasts to fake IDs, from augmentation to forgery. Some think fake plants are cheap or déclassé, impersonal or unsustainable. Some prefer to stick to "real plants," but the words "real" and "plant" aren't a natural pair. One of the meanings of "plant" is a false character, a disguised person, a spy. A plant lurks and collects information passively, hopes to go without being noticed at all. The plants of botany and horticulture don't plot against you (allegedly), and they aren't up to something (supposedly), so "plant" is the perfect costume for some kind of nonbotanical intelligence with an agenda. Still, unassuming, unthreatening, unintentional. Even as a verb, "plant" continues these clandestine operations in the phrase "planting a bug." On one hand, this seems to mean that you've placed a bug in the manner in which you place a plant in soil. On the other hand, maybe it means that you've turned the bug into a plant, turned something that might trigger a response into something more allaying. Stick bugs are an example of this in nature, whatever natural examples might be worth here.

"The plants are watching!" That was the paranoid motto of Jonathan Sarno's 1978 film, *The Kirlian Witness. The Kirlian Witness* follows a ficus whose telepathic skills are being investigated by a plant fanatic. Little meters are hooked up to leaves and, through electrochemical impulses, the plant seems to answer questions. When the plant fanatic is murdered, her sister steps in. Slowly, the laboratory ficus helps fanatic number two deduce the killer's identity. That plant-turned-primate knowledge makes the surviving sister the next target of the killer. Plants know too much, know something they shouldn't know, and something we absolutely shouldn't know either. We don't know how they know, or why they even care, which makes the whole thing more menacing. The plants are a few steps ahead of us, and once you've been duped, it's hard not to worry it'll happen again. I think we're a little suspicious of plants with their calm demeanor and seemingly detached air. All plants already register as a little fake.

And now my *Cryptanthus* was suspected of being a *plant* plant: a total fake, a fraud. Soon enough, a virus (who has had its own troubles with being "real") caused the library to lock its doors, with my office plants in position behind them. When I returned months later to pack up my things, the *Cryptanthus* had turned mostly brown. I prodded and coddled it at home, but no luck. I wondered whether the dry, tan remainders would've convinced the students that the plant was once alive. Can fake plants die? Months later still, I found a photo online that showed a table full of *Cryptanthus*, probably at a garden center or greenhouse. The overlaid text reads, "I'm not dead, this is just how I look." If my students had captioned my *Cryptanthus*, the text would probably say, "I'm not real, this is just how I look."

Just beyond the window of my lost office was another *plant* plant: a technological plant, in the form of cell phone towers molded to look like pines and palms. These phone trees are convincing if seen in the margins of the eye or from a dirty car window speeding down the road. In calling these plants "phone trees," I'm hoping to revive an extinct creature from decades before the mass text message. The phone tree feels like a false memory, but I know that next to the telephone of my youth was a list of numbers to be dialed—branches along the tree. Mary's husband would go into hospital, or the little girl who had been sick since birth would be herself, and we'd get a phone call.

Ring ring.

"Well, start praying," one middle-aged Midwestern woman would say to another. Her name was right above ours in the list. We'd pray with the caller, then hang up. Then we'd search the list for the name that followed our own.

"Well, start praying."

I don't want to pray anymore, but I'd love to hear the phone ring and know it's a friend with a prompt to find another.

Back in the Arizona desert, a passing wind susses out which trees are plants and which are *plants*, as the phone trees are left—like their telephone pole cousins—standing immobile against the weather. For those people who are paranoid about plants (fakes) in the environment, phone trees are the real *plant*. Internet preachers of techno terror hallucinate phone trees irradiating us into another genre of madness through a cocktail of 5G, EMF, and psyops waves. Techno death is cloaked in the beguiling disguise of "nature," nature being something given by God or maybe a debt we owe to the future or just a good place to relax. The government, or perhaps a shadow government, is making fools out of us with these plant plants—getting us to trust what will eventually kill us. Being vigilant against plants is the only hope. It's hard to know how to properly hate the phone tree from this paranoid vantage though. Is the phone tree just another dupe, playing into a nefarious hand and handing us over in turn? Is the phone tree nature gone wrong, earth elements conspiring against polluting humans to get a planet's revenge? These are paranoid questions, and maybe the phone tree is a paranoid object, created to give us a reason for the fear we already feel.

But what about 5G pine cones we can mount on our roofs? What about art installations of projected and sculpted "fires," burning and scarring the metallic evergreen growth? What about the possibility of living with phone trees through a feeling other than terror? These kinds of questions can't be reached through paranoia, because paranoia is a state of actively encircling something—a fear, a trauma, a wish—and being unwilling or unable to leave it. This is not the dancing orbit of a stone being twirled among planets but something more rigid, something with tracks. Adoration of fake plants, or plant fakery, is too far out for the paranoid. Maybe that's why I'm giving it a try. Sometimes, I grin, bite my tongue, hope to be tricked, hope to touch the little lines running tangent to a clean circle of narrative. Paranoid people want to bend those escapes back in and round off the whole matter, want to pick and plant the plants, want to know who's a phony and why and how. Better that cancer, AIDS, and COVID-19 should be caused by a false pine giving off truly transparent radiation than by opaque pathogens and biomechanical processes or—even worse—human malice. When I hear the question, "Is it a real plant?" I hear a confession, or an attempt to diffuse a fear by sharing it. I hear someone looking past the plant, of whatever sort it might be, back into themselves, onto their tracks, hunting themselves down.

You can hunt down *plants* all you like, but they'll still catch you in the end. Plastic tulips are lying on Grandpa's eternal recliner, the laziest boy, a box of some wood buried six feet deep. These synthesized flowers are made of a malleable matter, something agnostic about its final form. It didn't come directly from another plant, didn't have to be a plant. Could've been the ninety-nine-cent planter, a plant tag, a bag of Planters peanuts. Or perhaps it's better to say the matter didn't have to be a plant *again*. Pop's tulips may not have come from seed or cutting, from graft or rhizome, but the oil used to produce their polyester tissues is the remainder of ancient plants pressed into a sort of liquid fossil. Plants became materials that became plants again. It's a sort of transmogrification that folds back in on itself as a politically volatile product becomes an aesthetically denounced *thing* that stands in for political volatility. We buy cheap things because we're cheap people.

Any discussion of plastics in the twenty-first century is, rightfully, rooted in concerns of ecological wreckage. Spiderlike spinnerets create thin threads of oil-based polyester, which are then formed into sheets of fabric. Once cut and shaped, the polyester is grafted onto a stem containing a flexible iron skeleton. With this very posable mineral center, perhaps we try to make fake plants a little more like our own animal bodies. The lifespan of these flowers is expansive. In comparison to a human life, it's infinite. It persists and overtakes. The fake flower just won't die in a way we can see.

Most fake flowers are created in large factories, and labor conditions are probably—and we can just assume this now—not great. Crude-oil extraction and lousy work environments could prompt a news article, to which a blog would respond by filling in the story of how managers were forced to become managers. Colonization, the global demand for plastic flowers, Western cultures of eternal life and hidden death, suburban crafting society, and "flows of capital" could form dense sedimentary layers in scholarly monographs. It would all be very true and very real, and it would bend the lines of chance back into a circle of scholarship—scholarship that seeks to minimize the chance of getting the story wrong, telling a falsehood. So my most plantlike apologies to the scholars, the journalists, the activists, the revolution, and the messiah for what comes next.

Anyway—

to cut a fresh flower from its stalk, drown its wound in tap water, and abandon it to the center of a dining room table reserved for guests who you wish you'd never invited—

seems like a way to say:

"I really fucking hate these plants."

Cell divisions and gamete formations have pumped up anthers—pillowy biscuits dusted with yellow pollen—as a circle of charms around the sticky stigma of an egg-bearing ovary. Glints of sun have been devoured and soil microbes befriended, all with the plan of petals opening up to wind and bat and insect and spider as a statement of invitation and incitement. A flower: a grand finale, an uncontrollable exit from a growing season.

And then, those dull scissors in the kitchen win the honor of just cutting that show right from its stage. Dance for the guest, sweetie! Until the curtain falls, dance! And then it's out with the trash.

"I mean, have you ever, in all your life?!"

Then again, plants themselves hardly tend toward the eternal or sentimental. The oak hoards the ground and sky, putting shadowy hands to the task of strangling upstart sprouts. The same dominating leaves, the source of the tree's supremacy, are then sucked dry of nutrients and cast off in the shortening autumn days. Bougainvillea, a subtropical garden imperative, tosses fuchsia bracts on the ground like smoldering cigarettes for the ushering winds to sweep up. They litter driveways, easily mistaken for pastel candy wrappers. Numerous species of flowers—aptly termed "ephemerals"—have designed their lives to be lived in short weeks, bursting up and into flames of color without human eyes catching the light. Dandelions, meanwhile, string the sky with fine seeds, more than keeping up with the rapid turnover of their membership, brought on by grazing, mowing, spraying, and decaying. Humans may make seeds precious in Nordic mountains, but plants toss out hundreds or thousands in the knowledge that just a few will make it. The flower you've anxiously cut—hoping it will impress or console—may be replaced by another flower as stupendously replaceable as the last. Need I even mention the quantities of pollen falling carelessly out of pine cones? Plants ask their mothers what will they be, and Doris Day sings out: "*Que será será.*" If we are wasteful and reckless in forming flowers out of fossils, it's not out of line with the modus operandi of plants.

Hey, let's go back and look at those daisies again, yeah?

With all this in mind, shellacking a flower with junior high polish hardly seems like an offense. Whoever streaked the daisy's rays with glitter probably spent more time with that flower, more time intimately wandering its puckered structures, than anyone else, except the plant itself. Imagine a fine brush tucking into the flower's smaller secrets to spread glitter, which will not be seen until the flower desiccates and disassembles. The brush then flies outward past the edge of each ray as though it were continuing the flower invisibly. Unlike those of us who crouch over garden plants with acidic concern, the daisy painter goes beyond wallowing in the supposed perfection of phytoforms and takes a risk on contributing to the finished work. There is the risk of getting it wrong, of mucking it up, when you paint the daisy, but there's risk, too, in casting your seeds in a concrete parking lot and hoping something else will carry them to soft dirt.

Perhaps hand-brushing is unreasonable to expect nowadays, and instead adhesive was sprayed across whole fistfuls of flowers, then glitter tossed in warehouse air. Aleatory scatters of mirrored plastic form along floor and drop cloth, skin and clothing, ceiling and window. A wasteful process of throwing swine all over your pearls. Tacky, in all senses of the word. Catching, too. A chintzy spectacle, painting the daisy in this way asks for more sacrifice than hand-brushing, more wasted matter and more risk. Glitter exposes human membranes and tissues to cutting edges, just as the flowering plant was once exposed and cut. Airborne glues trouble the lungs and irritate the skin. If there's something to be gained in glittering the daisy, there's something to be lost as well. Perhaps we ought to take up daisy painting in our homes, sitting solitary under evening lamps with gluey fingertips snagging on blanket threads, and glitter stuck to our teeth (how and why will never be sure). I think, when we go back to the question of the painted daisy, we'll find that plants might not disapprove.

Oh, and let's stop by the cemetery on our way.

On the tomb of an unknown soldier, a go-go boy, a backdoor barfly, is a clutch of Gerbera daisies decorated with sovereign glitter—the floral emblem of the consequence of life.

Fake plants, whether forgeries, adulterations, or the wrongly accused, are a human tactic for responding to botanical forms we did not, could not, make, forms made under the intensity of botanical being. The plants that flourish from seed or bulb, which photosynthesize or (in the case of parasitic plants) suck sap from their prey—we cannot create them. No artisan device or clever technological craft can combine earth elements to form plant life as we know it in forests and botanical gardens. Plant breeders may endlessly fine-tune the surface morphology and seasonal acts of a flower, but they cannot build the being cell by cell. The plant must lend itself to human shaping.

The fake plant's foes write that we abandon the real when we turn to fake plants. We give up on cooperating with nature in favor of something entirely (supposedly) within our own control, the line goes. It seems to me, though, that we confess an almost embarrassing indebtedness to the plants that inspire us when we make fake plants. We take a leap by trying to recreate in static form something that is pulsating with sap, composed of layers of minuscule cells, each doing something or another inside their provincial walls. The plants against which fake plants are judged are busily engaged with everything around them. Fake plants do not attempt to mimic this level of structure and movement, do not muscle in on the micro-fungal-phyto-faunal pathways of forest ferns' being, but instead mirror back the broad elements of phytoforms at a given time. Through fake plants, we turn our attachment to the world into an image. Rapturous affection, disclosed through analogy.

Fake plants are a tribute. Like any tribute, the fake plant may stray far from the register of known traits and accepted botanical facts. In these excursions, new genius may emerge—or embarrassing failure: an artless portrait of a lover. And who's to blame? The unappealing contours of a fake plant cannot be added to the Almighty's aesthetic tab or blushingly excused as Darwinian "fitness." If you make an ugly fake plant, it's *you* who made it. The fake plant is the risk of getting it wrong, maybe even *hoping* to get it wrong from time to time. Fake plants are a sign of trying to be human, specifically, painfully human, in a busy world of incomprehensible creatures we admire, for whom we hold tender affection and great awe. I imagine plants staring us down eyelessly as we fret over what's real and what's not, releasing words from their pores. "You're not real, it's just how you look."

For those who've already greenhoused their apartments, perhaps it's time to plant plastic plants that evoke the less-salable possibilities: kudzu, Japanese smartweed, Tree of Heaven, pigweed, poison ivy. These are the green invaders, the unscratchable itches, the suffocating botanical surplus. Though we cannot—or perhaps will not—grow their wild forms by volition, we can plant the plastic versions in our homes and gardens. These are portraits of new forbidden lovers. Plant diseases too. Imagine silk corn smut, a faux infection whose words keep double-dipping into plantiness.

In my own yard, I often choose patches where I allow "weeds" to grow large and free, to see what they become and what they do. Bitter stalks of prickly lettuce (*Lactuca serriola*) become four-foot-tall curves topped by rayed white flowers busy with insects. Puncture vine *(Tribulus terrestris)* intergrows with Arizona poppy (*Kallstroemia grandiflora*), forming a lush mat of green sprinkled with tiny yellow flowers and big, operatic shouts of gold. Cheeseweed mallow leaves (*Malva parviflora*) provide a sort of pointillist repetition of green dots across a dirt patch, varying in height and size. In online gardening groups, images of these plants are often posted with the question, “Is this a wildflower?” Respondents write back, “No, it’s a weed.” Weeds too, you see, are fake plants of a kind. So it only makes sense that we form our portraits of them in silk and velvet and clay, pack them around the usual hostas and *Monstera* and tomatoes. I imagine careful gridlines of plastic dandelions planted through heritage rose gardens, and potted glass crabgrass sitting on front porch steps.

Buy painted daisies, too. I go back again and again to the painted daisies in my mind, wondering who painted them, bought them. How many faces lived shimmered moments of reflection across the dots of glitter? I want to go back and buy them, live with them, watch them decay, or seal them in resin. I want to take more photos and let the camera clonally reproduce their rootless bodies, let the flowers feed the camera the doubt it desires.

PART III
IMAGES

Snowy

All video is a loop, an option to return to. A door double-marked "exit" and "entrance." And so I revisit a particular performance, once on VHS tape and now digital, again and again and again to pass a landmark I know but can never quite remember on my own.

In 1989, a drag queen named Snowy competed in the Miss Pittsburgh pageant at Pegasus nightclub in the city's downtown. Her winning performance, recorded on tape for the absent, gives a charmingly suspect sketch of the evening. Suspect because, having been to Pegasus myself in the early 2000s, I know how much space rests behind the camera tripod, how many dark corners go unseen, how many interactions with bartenders are unheard. What's missing is charming. It invites us to contribute—like a party guest asked to bring liquor, lust, fucking, fighting, terminal cigarettes, and ice. I'm excited by what the camera misses. It gives me something to say. I return to this video again and again, just to see Snowy's performance.

The tape begins.

No, not quite. What begins is a digitization of a VHS tape, though the French word—*numérisation*—tells us more. The tape's contents have been digitized, numeritized, turned into numbers for calculation on a computer. But on that night in 1989, sensors in a VHS camera received light and sound signals from the fray at Pegasus and inscribed them by repositioning little magnetic zones on strips of plastic tape. The tape rolled across the camera's recording head continuously in tandem with the outlaying of time in space—unflinching, gluttonous. What it wrote down is a scroll of sorts. Distance from the start of the reel stands in for distance from the start of an interval of time. Or maybe it's the tape that turns time into intervals. In recording or playback, the tape is followed in a linear fashion, from one plastic spool to another. A tape can always be fast-forwarded or rewound, but jumping directly to one area or another is impossible. A VHS deck reads the scroll aloud.

But VHS is not what I am watching. What I am watching is this scroll turned into a series of interlocking self-references, ones and zeros in a matrix, reading chapters one and four and half the index at the same time: a digital video. Inside the digital video file are all sorts of dates other than that night in 1989: the day the tape was digitized in our hot Arizona living room, the moment when the file arrived on my device, the cooked-up nostalgic instant when I last opened it. Even the file itself isn't a single thing. The icons I double-click lead me to think that somewhere on my laptop is a single zone that contains all the words I've typed into this manuscript. The data are actually scattered across available spots on my hard drive. What I double-click is more like a set of actionable instructions for assembly. I am watching entries pulled from an index: rapid reference. The VHS scroll was sampled in digitization. Representative bits were taken out of the scroll, made to stand in for lost time. I'm watching something altogether different from the VHS tape created when Snowy was there, then copied over and over again. Each VHS copy lost or transposed details. Each play, rewind, fast-forward, each time the tape was left played halfway through, the plastic tape stretched and wrinkled, the coatings demagnetized, becoming both substrate and content, setting a new date in the future, a last play date. A VHS tape only allows you to exit and return so many times. A digital video? How many returns does it permit?

The video begins. Three backup dancers step-march from the left of the camera frame, legs and arms clenched in programmed movements that look unsure but hopeful. As leather jackets above, so light blue denim below. Video does not tell me the texture in this instance, but the denim seems supple and cooperative. These are not new pants. Following in short order is a taller woman in a simple gold-sequined cocktail dress. Her head turns to the beat of Tina Turner's "Addicted to Love," and she—Snowy—entices the camera to zoom toward her. Lyrics begin, and lithe hands gesture: open palm against side of head, open palm with fingers gliding across collarbone, open palm gathering a kiss and pushing it on video waves away. Steps to the left lead to a spin back toward the right and VHS reveals its hidden glory. The camera sensor is overloaded by the glare of a sequin

which is—I think—the maddened glare of the gods when they strike us with fortune or failure and

which is—I think—the maddened glare of a person challenged with the impossible.

A sequin offers a glimpse of the infinite we cannot bear to witness in its entirety, an infinity that necessitates breaking every camera everywhere. Vision cracks and sizzles, the eye burns away like a strip of film lingering in front of the projector bulb. It's all going away now: no one passes, and no one matters, and no one survives until the end. All this from a plastic circle on a cocktail dress, because it is density and refusal that count.

What have we wrought, this world where weather girls have pores and the toupees of game-show hosts glow with a plastic shame? We must thank, must bless the obsolete camera as the mechanical eye that perceives images of imbalance, of excess, and translates them into a glare. The VHS camera, working in a dark corner of a late-night gay function does not promise layers we can extricate and catalog. It melts down, slag and ore and plasticity all fused in an everything-nothing. All the questions come alive again. Obfuscation creates the fecundity desire requires. It's the shadow a mushroom grows in.

Gasp, why don't you.

Shards of light refract parallel to Snowy's torso, across her face and head, as though she were being crowned by the visible spectrum. Lyrics roll on, and Snowy misses a dance cue.

There are many reasons to smile when you miss a cue in a performance. I don't know why Snowy smiles here. She smiles, and my eyes are zoomed like the camera, back onto her and always onto her.

I can't feel anyone here with me in this moment about Snowy. Good drag is an aching illusion: only you and the performer exist in the universe, and you can't help but feel this is a complete arrangement. Nothing else is needed or wanted. It turns out beauty was the meaning of life, glamour its fullest expression. Good drag is rare, but all drag is a seductive suggestion of a break. Sequins, wigs, makeup, lashes, tape, garments, props, dancers, lights, music, shoes, flippers, boas, tear-aways all in service of *maybe*. One day, we will find that drag was only ever about gender insofar as gender is the obliteration of oneself in collision.

I worry I am making too much out of one performance. I fear that I will embarrass myself by writing about sequins

which are most unspeakably powerful

as the spectral entities they are. I will reveal myself to be the insubstantial faggot I'm suspected of being. The worry is a want rephrased: let me become insubstantial, unserious, a dilettante with false lashes. What thought has a faggot except the thought to die from and in a glare?

Snowy smiles after missing a step. Crouching, pivoting, pointing along with the music, her backup dancers are pinky fingers daintily following the shimmering index as best they can.

On auto-focus, the camera loses track of its focal point, and Snowy—in a head-and-shoulders shot—is blurred. As the image recedes, I crane my neck toward the computer hoping to manipulate an optical situation almost thirty years past. Some air is held on reserve in my lungs while I wait. A rush of data spreads itself on my screen, and Snowy's visage returns, her forearm framing a backup dancer's head as she leans back to caress his face.

He's hers now, like Tina said.

She smiles a loss of control. A horse is midhurdle. Good drag is between the video frames, and maybe that is why it is so hard to describe. Maybe the move to the realm of the digital was inevitable because we, too, are sampling creatures in our conscious lives. We do not, in full awareness, grasp the brunt of sensation constantly undulating toward us at all times, but those undulations reverberate in our unconscious minds.

Maybe you've seen the video of the gorilla on the basketball court? It's an old psychological demonstration. Four or six or some number of people are playing basketball and someone—a professor or a researcher or a friend—asks the viewer to count how many passes the numbered players make. In the midst of the plays, a person in a gorilla suit emerges from off-screen and dances midscene. For the viewer who concentrates on the basketball in motion, the mind filters out the gorilla. You don't see it. It misses you.

The conscious mind is a sample of all the shakes passing by, but we desire what evades the sample. Drag is a fullness of time, analog, and when we concentrate on it, we begin to feel the ever-flowing, ever-rusting creeks of iron oxide on tapes somewhere not so far away. Drag is a return of runoff and waste. Did we digitize our tapes so we could want them all the more, so we could heighten the desire to have been there or to be there again? Digitization as a wish for abandonment.

When I pause the video, Snowy's hands are splayed across the interlacing fields and I get a birds-eye view of a jagged pyramid. Thinner at the edges, denser toward the center, lines extending with uncertainty. Which part is palm, is finger, is nail? I resume the video, and for a few moments, Snowy generates the music around her without effort. Then Tina resurges, as shaky choreography brings the pinky-heavy hand of Snowy into dance-line formation. The line changes orientation from clockwise to counterclockwise. The line becomes points.

Eyes alight, is there anything behind them?

Is my mind even mine?

Snowy is the attracting pulse of good drag. It's a pulse that simultaneously promises an impossible closeness while making unbearably apparent how separate we are from others. We wish to become another, to dissolve our independence and flow into confederacy. It's an impossibility, and we're better for it. We all want to emit that pulse, to have that power of attraction. Activists might rally a community together, but it is performers who lend desire to intimacy. Activists seek to extend life in time, but what does it matter if there is no drag, if there is no living?

The final verse of the song parallels the first, and I come to realize Snowy is repeating choreography. It is a bodily chant: fist, fist, pull-thrust. Each cliché, each seeming error tilts the surface between Snowy and me, and I roll toward her. One backup dancer lip-synchs along with Snowy. Another looks like a frightened version of Cornflake S. Pecially, from *Mister Rogers' Neighborhood*.

Mystery gives way to busyness, and I begin to wonder about the remaining runtime. A cold draft touches below my neck and distracts me from the final minute of the video—more dancing, Snowy lifted aloft by her pinkies—and I decide to watch the video again from the beginning. Performance spits out pieces of time that are their own destruction. Video allows me to return again and again to Snowy's performance, but it's harder to stay with her. My mind wanders here and there. I return to see what I missed on my last visit. I can never really remember what I saw the last time I was here. I return to the video and complete the loop. I unfold time compressed into a video file and let that expansion compress my awareness of my surroundings, my anxiety, my faggy problems. This maneuver will reverse as the video closes and the surrounding world reinflates. I will return to Snowy again.

Is my mind even mine?

Watch Snowy for yourself, courtesy of the Pittsburgh Queer History Project: www.danilamorte.com/snowy

Against the Shutter

"Take a picture. It'll last longer."

I type the phrase above and look across the street. A man in a cerulean button-down and khakis is staring at me from under a gray baseball hat. An embroidered monarch butterfly sits in the gray. I'm sitting in the shadow of a statue on a bright April day, planning to use sunny 16.

"Sunny 16" is a camera setting. On a sunny day, set the camera's aperture to 1/16th. Then set the shutter speed to the inverse of the film speed: ISO 100 becomes 1/100th of a second. Maybe that's all jargon to you, but that's how I've set my camera today, and that's how the butterfly man set his too. Neither of us knows that. Neither of us knows the other has a camera. His camera bag is kept out of sight by the car next to which he's standing. My camera is tucked inside the book bag at my side. He doesn't know I'm sitting here to write about cameras, and I don't know—not yet—that he wants to take my photo. I'm just thinking, Why is he staring at me?

He crosses the street and starts saying the words I'm already thinking: camera, light, lens, sunny, sixteen, film, photo. Nobody's psychic. We just happen to have the same problem. It's a photographic disorder, a way the camera makes us act all funny, all out-of-sorts. We don't want to get better though. We keep buying cameras, taking photos, sharing them around. It's a common disease. I bet you have it too.

Over the better part of an hour, butterfly cameraman and I trade some thoughts on our troubles.

"Cameras are too precise now."

"They capture too much detail."

"I don't need to see the capillaries on a stranger's face."

I tell him about my obsession with cyanotype—a nineteenth-century photographic method and the original method of making blueprints—about how slow and unpredictable it is. He tells me that you can take the lens out of a 1990s Xerox copy machine and make interesting images with it. He's got a busted camera waiting for him in his car. It just arrived from eBay and has a sensor chip filter that he needs in order to fix a different camera. I'd be lying if I said I knew exactly how a digital camera works. I know enough to follow along sincerely though. I think about the cameras I've bought for parts or just to look inside them. There are so many cameras now, so many versions of "taking a photograph." For some people, their disease sits behind the camera and looks through the lens. For others, it's in front of the lens. Some of us are sick the whole time we travel through the lens, from seer to seen and back again.

My first self-portrait was a four-by-six-inch photograph taken in a simple Minolta 35mm camera, sometime around the age of ten. Alone in my bedroom, I draped an old bedsheet, decorated with a yellow floral print, onto the curtain rod of my window. In front of my backdrop, I placed a yellow-seated step stool that bore splashes of white latex wall paint. I posed myself, along with my favorite yellow teddy bear, on the step stool after activating the camera's self-timer. Not yet understanding photographic framing, or the somewhat misleading results of putting eyeglassed eyes up to a viewfinder, I expected to create a tightly framed image: torso, teddy, yellow flowers. I saw what I planned to see. I clicked the button, rewound the film, and mailed the roll out of town for developing. What returned weeks later was a nearly full-body image with wide wings of surrounding wall. The bedsheet was apparent as a bedsheet. Hemmed edges and care instruction tags. The paint splatters across the ripped yellow seat were a rearrangement of my smile. I looked as poor and lonely as I was. The image I'd imagined through the camera and what the camera imagined back were tangential to one another.

Photographic portrait studios of the mid-1800s often had furniture and decor offerings with which the sitter could choose to pose. A nice wingback leather chair and a hardcover leather tome for your man-of-the-mind fantasy, perhaps. Portraits attempt to condense what's otherwise scattered throughout disparate dreams. Over time, and borrowing from painting, portrait photography has formed a sort of language. The words are poses, blocks of light, lassitudes of focus. I have trouble saying, in the language of photography, what a photograph of me should look like. I know what previous photographs already look like, but somehow I'm not understood by the camera when I rephrase my wants.

What do you want from a photo of yourself? I know what I want: a running creek, water sloshing in a bucket, a searing indigo edge, one of those prime-time over-the-shoulder glimpses selling flavored instant coffee or celebrity scent. Tweed but only on Katharine Hepburn. A beard but only on me, only some of the time. Drapes of linen that have never touched the floor, and some garden dirt under oval-cut nails. Someone who gets up from a theater seat *perfectly*. Someone who smiles effortlessly. An echo of my fantasies. A participant in my dreams. Everything I want from a photograph is what a photograph doesn't do. What I want flickers on the lip of a puddle.

When I look at myself in the mirror, light bends at the outer edges of my eyeglasses. It washes hazy in the margins of my attention. There's so much movement, supple and tender, as mirror and eyes and face all reposition in response to each other. With two mirrors, I try to see the back of my head but distance, smeared glass, and the limitations of a line of sight muddle things. I'm glimpsing, averaging out more than seeing clearly. I accept this, knowing that the friends and strangers who see me are not perfected vision machines. They're as unclear as I am.

Their inattentions, half-fantasies, ocular impairments, allergenic mucous excretions all get in the way of "seeing clearly." When others see me, I'm moving around, and so any angle which is a "bad angle" is temporary and unlikely to be held for long. Sight can be sympathetic. In the live moment, you and I are too percussed by sensory apparitions, external and internal, to study up close what only lasts seconds. I love that about vision: things mistaken, made-up, and only seen in memory.

In the printed photograph, though, we find what Hervé Guilbert called a "second fovea." The fovea, you might remember from high school health class, is the dense concentration of cones in a pit at the center of a retina. It's where vision is sharpest, a zenith of visual acuity. The photograph is like a whole moment fallen into the ditch of the eye, forever sharp and vivid in its own ways. It's stuck in the ditch, not going anywhere. We can trace it out slowly, repetitively. Guilbert describes this as a fingertip gently caressing an image: no distance, all truth.

The too-true photograph that my Minolta produced is something to which I've become habituated. These are images made for objectivity. Records and documents. Verifications. Testimonies. Things that speak on my behalf, that tell me to mind my manners, keep my mouth shut, the photo is not done speaking. I still have the photo somewhere but I never take it out. I just retrace the memory of seeing it, a sort of photograph in of through for the mind. I keep it as a reminder of what happened that day. That was the day I got shut up in the gelatin, in the sticky surface of a photographic print. I know you'll think I'm dramatic if I call it a tragedy, but don't you know that's precisely what I'm going for here?

Take a picture. It'll last longer.

The "it" of "it'll last longer" is the photograph, which always lasts longer than the taking. That's my photography problem: time and its tenses. In his treatise on photography, *Camera Lucida*, Roland Barthes thinks on photography as a technology of evidence, demonstrating that something *has been*. There's a certain commonsense logic to his thinking: if you see a photograph of something, something must've existed somewhere at some time for its likeness to have been captured by a camera. Myself, I wouldn't make a claim quite so grand. Many things can complicate the relationship between a photo and what "was there": lens flares, optical illusions, grains in the film emulsion. At best, a photograph demonstrates that a camera existed. More specifically, some kind of photochemistry (some kind of chemistry that responds to light) exists. A photograph indicates that the world is receptive, reactive. If the photograph is evidence of anything, it's evidence of what that reactivity means to us.

Barthes loved the hard bang of the shutter opening and closing to "take" a photo. In this insisting sound, I hear the gavel striking a verdict. But verdicts instigate new series of options. We can appeal, concede, celebrate, complain, or even mount a jailbreak. Maybe jailbreak is the right analogy because, in a jailbreak, you magnify your problem. You're free, but all the forces that want to imprison you double their strength.

Let's look more closely at the camera, get up against it. Etymologically, *against* derives from *again,* emphasized with *-st.* It's not just one action or two, but an open quantity. There are many emphatic, repetitive pressures against the camera: finger on button, dust on lens, light on film.

You know how, when you get too close to the camera, maybe with your face or with your fingertip on the lens, you can't make a good image?

Let's make bad images. Come on, let's move up against the camera, too close to make any good evidence.

Look back through the camera lens, like you're the picture-taking apparatus now, scrutinizing with lenses of water rather than glass. If your reflection appears behind the glass of the lens, that's because you're looking into a small mirror sitting just behind it. The mirror is positioned like a person who's resting against a wall, shoulders to the plaster and feet projected forward. Your eye is closest to the foot. You'll see the same mirror if you look through the camera's viewfinder, shouting back whatever it's got on the other side of the lens. When you depress the shutter release button, the button that "takes" the photo, the mirror swings up and lays flush against the top of the camera. Now, staring into the lens, you can see that something was behind the mirror: a curtain. How theatrical! Louis Jacques Mandé Daguerre, who made some of the first permanent photographs in the late 1830s, also designed sets for stage productions. His cameras didn't have little mirrors and curtains, but maybe our cameras do because he's gone.

According to photography guides, the curtain you see is something called a "focal plane shutter." When the mirror flips up, the curtain slides out of the way and lets light flow to the camera's protected possession: the film. We see the movement in sound: WHACK-CRUNCH. In some fraction of a second, things open and then close again. The mirror falls and the curtain slides, and together they seclude the strip of film once more. The shutter denies the film what it responds to. The image is *made*. Past tense. Verdict reached. The lens stays open and the film stays reactive, but the shutter keeps them apart.

A shutter is that which closes, seals up, prevents wild, metastatic change. A window shutter breaks a line of vision that would otherwise stitch the indoors and the outdoors into one another. An exterior shutter guards the window glass from being broken by flying tree branches, lover's rocks. The interior shutter—what might it hold back? Palms banging, messaging out to be free? We shutter to think what they would say. A shutter is a shudder, a shaking and a clenching. When you shudder, don't you close your eyes, crumple up your neck, try to shut out the sensation that overwhelms you? The camera shudders twice: once breaking itself free from its sensory torpor (opening the shutter) and a second time returning to it (closing it again). When the shutter shuts, I lose touch with the sensitized film loaded into the camera. A crunch-shuffle sound advances the film forward and the live moment of sensation shared between me and the inverted image of my light, impressed on the film, is split in two. I'm burdened with being unauthoritatively live; the photo with being authoritatively dead.

The shutter is an anatomical concern, perhaps a callus on the finger. It's an insensitivity. Roland Barthes thought the finger was the most photographic organ. After all, it's the finger depressing the shutter release, triggering mechanical movements, which leads to the capture of an image. Whatever the eye might have seen through the viewfinder, whatever the photographer's vision may have recognized and selected in framing, is made into a recorded decision through the finger's downward movement. If the finger holds the shutter open too long, an unclear image will result. The finger might ruin it all. We've all made those photos, marks of indecision, insecurity, insensitivity, uncertainty, unpreparedness, unreadiness, untidiness, undulation, undying, undoing, daring, dancing, damming and damning, daydreaming, dallying, dithering, wandering, waffling, wavering, waxing, wasting, waning, wanting, walling up, walling off, walking off, walking out, wishing about something else somewhere else at some other time.

The opening of the shutter is a response to a pressing finger. When the shutter closes, it's because the finger has withdrawn. In isolation, an image thickens and hardens. I know that, when he said that the finger was the most photographic organ, Barthes meant that the finger is the most important organ in the scheme—but I can't help also reading him as saying that the finger is the most *photogenic* organ. Most photographic, as in "best suited to the camera." The eye wants to see the finger at least as much as the finger wants to touch the eye.

"Fingeryeye"—this is what Eva Hayward calls the jointed, synesthetic organ by which we perceive texture not as something *out there* but always inside/outside, always formed in the moment of touch between you *in here* and that something *out there*. That moment forms the you-something here-there, too. This isn't the anatomy you learned in high school, so don't be bashful if you've never heard of this sense. Eva writes of touching cup corals in a marine lab where she conducted research. Her duties included cleaning and sexing these little oceanic beings. As she pushed her fingers into the water-filled lab containers where the corals lived, she watched the water bend the image of her hand. Her hand, sensing the body of the water, worked in tandem with her eye to find its movement and touch the corals. The water was somewhat alien to her, homely to them. Touch and sight continually surpassed one another, as her fingers telegraphed through her body the probing reach of the curious corals. It's not the finger doing the work and not the eye. It's something else, a "fingeryeye." It's always open and feeling, but awareness of this organ comes and goes, like a muscle you can't feel until it aches.

In Eva's case, she ached for these eyeless corals who know the world through the continual touch of water. Nothing about them, the corals or the non-corals, had any kind of image in that moment except through the water, through the air, in the touch, from the light, all at once. Often, we mistake vision for distance and touch for intimacy, but the fingeryeye makes us recognize how close and far at once we always are to what we encounter. We are the encounter.

This isn't so far from what Guilbert describes in his essay on the fovea. If you hold your arm out straight, the fovea accounts for an area in the field of vision approximately the size of your pinky fingernail. The fovea, Guilbert opines, is like a little finger tracing out the things we look at, touching them intimately. Memories of that intimacy drift outward to form the less clear, perhaps semi-imagined texture of peripheral vision. The (sharp) photographic print forms a "second fovea," a concentration of ever-sharp vision that we can erotically caress and that ordinarily does not change (perceptibly) before our eyes. In his way, Guilbert suggests that vision can be understood through touch. The glance is never innocent, but other organs might wish it so. Looking is presumptive, invasive, immediate. Obsessive. Barthes feared the photographer's eye and preferred to think on the finger as the photographic organ. But if he thought he could get away from the eye by paying attention instead to the finger, Eva's encounters with cup corals demonstrate that the eye and finger were never working separately in the first place. Barthes refused to write as a photographer, as the person behind the camera, and so he couldn't have known the mistake he was making in imagining he could displace either finger or eye. They're always sharing, trading, sending impressions back and forth.

It's Eva who diagnosed me as having a "photography problem." In an essay on photography, painting, and transsexuality, Eva pushes back against what she calls a "photo-ontic": a way of thinking that allows the photograph to speak to what is real, what succeeds or fails to become. Consider the before/after photo layout that tells us so-and-so is *now* a woman, now that the camera can capture that sort of likeness on her. It's a way of thinking that treats the transsexual as a surface, a static something which can be detailed from the outside. It denies all the churning, swashing, rippling, pouring, streaming, steaming life that happens in realms where the eye needs a chaperone or a companion. In the logic of the photo-ontic, the transsexual does not exist for herself, only for the camera to assert more mastery. The camera can see anything, decide the truth of anything. You'll take the photo far too literally, and *she* will lose out.

When Eva talks about a photography problem, I think she means it as something like a drinking problem—an addiction to the camera. I have that problem. But a problem is also an irritant, like a stomach problem. I'm also irritated by all these camera-made photographs supposedly of me. I keep going back to them anyway. Repetition on repetition. When I see these fixed images, I find out that I don't mean to come together in front of the lens. I'm disassembling myself through the camera, the same way I'm asking you to look back through it and take it apart. I don't mean to be camera-ready.

I think I see a way out.

But then I see a camera, and I forget. I think I have to smile so you can see that I've become it now. Finally. *So sorry to have kept you waiting.*

WHACK-CRUNCH.

I've got a pit in the stomach of my eye.

Why do we understand vision as a sharpness of truth, when the breaths of our bodies refuse to be seen except in implication? We want, so badly, for our life sciences and dead gods to tell us, "*This is what is*," with each word italicized, Meisner-style, so we can go back and practice the stresses we want to feel. Against this, I am no match for my own camera-remade image. If you are presented with a camera-formed photograph of me, you will take it far too literally. You will use it as a heuristic for determining if something is or isn't me, if I've changed or remained the same. You will use it in all manner of authentication. Think of biometric scanners at national borders. If a photograph doesn't "look like me," you'll describe the mismatch as unexpected, but you probably won't consider it evidence *against* the camera in general. It's an aberration, not part of the history of photography. Maybe, though, now that you're here, you'll consider that some of us may be poor subjects for the camera, among us the television screen, the firework, the UFO, the prism paths along an eyelash. Our images are things of the amnesic now. I've seen myself most clearly outside the camera, searing in the indigo edge of a rectangle. The blue rectangle was part of a cyanotype.

Cyanotype is a photographic method, invented in the 1840s, and a technology for inversion. A mixture of two chemicals—ferric ammonium citrate and potassium ferricyanide—is applied to paper or something else using brushes, droppers, any tool that will distribute the liquid. The paper dries in minimal light and then is exposed, laid bare to the sun, thrown chemically open, made to play out its possibilities in front of our eyes. One chemical takes the role of the labile correspondent, inflamed by the sun's suggestions. The other chemical goes out in sympathy, creating an indissoluble blue. Any area of the paper hidden from the sun remains quiet. Exposure takes fifteen, twenty minutes or more. After exposure, the paper is washed for a few minutes, turning the exposed areas dark blue and leaving the sheltered areas white.

For about a month, not long after the pandemic began, I tracked a path from my kitchen to my patio, carrying long strips of paper treated to rectangles of chartreuse photochemistry. I laid the strips on the ground, shifted them through the path of the Arizona sun for ten or twenty minutes, then rinsed them in a basin. Nothing to cover up the reactive mix except the occasional passing cloud.

And then, one day, it was me. The blue rectangle floating in the plastic tub, bearing the slightest trace of a shift in sunlight, bore an unmistakable, unbearable resemblance to the me I try to know. I tried, in text now deleted, to explain this recognition. I can't. All the words scatter, as I suspect they would if I asked you to explain how you recognize yourself in a camera-made photograph. It's a matter of habituation or patterned feeling. It's why you can't see yourself getting old on a day-by-day basis. It's the uncanny of the bad haircut. You're always seeing with something other than "eyes." Maybe fingeryeyes, or a wish for a foot in the world.

To recognize myself, I wet my hands in the sun. I stare at a Prussian blue that looks back at me. I fall into a ditch of time. I smell ozone on a hot brick. I hear water that never knew a lonely Sunday.

Images in Plastic

Keep your vaccine card safe, inside sheets of plastic melted to the paper's surface like an American cheese slice that's finally lost the fiction of its separation from the wrapper. It's for bouncers who check the age of your body and antibodies. It's for doctors of tomorrow's decades piecing together how you've stayed alive. It's for whoever mucks out your stall at the end. It's for the future. It's an archive.

In one lineage of thought, an archive is anything into which streams of memory are concretized, treated as a reference point. Documents en masse are archives, as are old crown moldings, matchbooks spent and saved, practiced gestures of the Martha Graham technique, a sneeze. It's a poetic take on the archive made possible by something more useful, if less beautiful: the archivist's definition of "archive."

Distinguishing the poetic from the programmatic is the goal of Michelle Caswell's 2016 article, "'The Archive' Is Not an Archives: On Acknowledging the Intellectual Contributions of Archival Studies." Practiced sneezes and wet matches are all well and good, Caswell says, but what about the concrete archives—of nations and associations and universities and riverside boroughs—made of brick and stone and filled beyond capacity with documents? If an archive might be anything at all that evokes a memory, or encourages you to make one up from whole cloth, where does that leave the professional archivist who toils to keep Washington's diaries from commingling with

Franklin's albums? What about the person who photocopies your driver's license, ushers you past unarmed guards, brings you to boxes full of old phone books and inaccurate town maps? (If you've never had the pleasure of dissociating at the security checkpoints of an archive, this is a bit of what you're missing.)

Archivists struggle to be seen. In the late 1800s and early 1900s, when "archivist" solidified into a profession separate from "fancy man with paper," that second word in my facetious phrase was key. Archivists were mostly men. Those archivists, by all accounts, felt seen and empowered to set the theory and practice of working in archives. For complicated reasons, best explained by the sociologist I am not, these gendered demographics shifted in the late twentieth century, and now many archivists are women or, at least, not exactly men. For other complicated reasons, some systemic and some idiosyncratic, those archivists of today often feel unseen and unappreciated. According to Caswell, part of the problem is that the word "archive" has split into layers like wet plywood. Archivists feel invisible, and now the very noun at the core of their identity is moving away from them. They're *ists* without an archive.

There's nothing stable about the archive, whichever definition you choose. A laminated vaccination card is made of unstable, thin plastic which inundates cheap paper stock with adhesive. Each part is ready to rot and eggs on the others. Chemical byproducts of paper degradation are trapped under the plastic, and the plastic's own disintegration is stuffed into the paper fibers. They're teens in a TV scare-'em-straight movie forcing each other to drink while they drive while they smoke while they make prank calls while they have sex while they drop out of school to ride the trains. *Everything's going faster. We're gonna crash.*

The very fact that anyone laminates documents at home is itself a sort of accident. It's a bad idea from someone else's confused mind. Eddie Woodward writes that archives began laminating documents as early as the 1930s, using materials and processes different from the at-home setups you see today. Each year, methods changed slightly. With each change came new complications and disappointments in the outcome of lamination. Documents might yellow or scorch. Removing a document from an earlier enclosure, to put it in an updated one, could damage the document further. As early as the 1950s, there was serious doubt that lamination would ever improve the stability of documents. Everyone tinkered around with their lamination methods, though, trying to get all the good of plastic without the bad. Rhyme or reason for the practice was "altogether hazy" to some, including James L. Gear, chief chemist with the Document Restoration Branch at the National Archives. In the late 1980s, the practice was "put out of its misery," according to Woodward. Polymer-pulp materials of heritage were scattered across repositories, huffing chemical last breaths. In the meantime, the public picked up the habit and started outfitting birth certificates, death certificates, gift certificates with plastic futures.

"What does it mean to put a document under shiny plastic, make it all wet and troubled with extinction?" That's the most engaging way I can rephrase my old "research program"—the area of things I read and thought about as an academic archivist.

Yes, I know, listen. I get it. I didn't tell you I used to be an academic archivist. Fine, OK, and now I'm not even telling you what an academic archivist is. OK, yes. But

and you probably know this by now

this is how I get into jobs and images and gardens and television screens: I see something that isn't quite there, and then I really believe it, at least for a little while. Anyway.

I wanted to understand all the fallings apart of historical things. All those documents had been drowned in plastic, all involved parties "hazy" on why it went on for so long.

I began my research by attempting to destroy a photograph. The photograph in question showed two older ladies, neither of whom I knew, standing in front of a sign commemorating a 1978 golf event outside of Tucson. I picked up the photo at First Rate, Second Hand, a now-defunct thrift shop on Tucson's East

Side. That's also where we purchased a driftwood menorah that caught fire on the first night of Hanukkah. The menorah had little metal and leather cowboy ornamentations. We shaved down Shabbos candles to make them fit the tiny cups. Not long after sundown on the first night of Hanukkah, the whole thing was going up in flames on our dining room table. It wasn't meant to be. Charred, the menorah was moved outside and reclassified from holiday to garden decor.

The photograph was a lot less ostentatious than the menorah, I thought. It was a matte four-by-six-inch photograph with rounded corners. Blue dyes in the photograph had decomposed, giving the image a red cast. On the back of the image, someone had written "Irma Harrison" in blue ink. At first, I thought those were the names of the two women depicted. Harrison, my Harrison, perhaps as a result of their name, had an intuitive sense that I was wrong. "Irma Harrison" was one name, for just one of the women.

I knew nothing about Irma Harrison or the unnamed woman when I decided to destroy that particular photograph. In fact, I chose to destroy the photo because it *wasn't* very meaningful to me. Think along the lines of testing out a pen on an old bill envelope, or swatching paint on the wall behind a hutch. The first pancake. For my "research program," I would destroy the photograph and journal its destruction. I would learn something about the falling apart of historical things, trapped under plastic, or trapped under forgetting, or trapped under the forces to come as this old world turns red.

I put the photo in a plant pot on a table in my Tucson backyard, not far from the menorah-turned-conflagration-turned-yard-ornament. Rooted next to the photo was an *Opuntia* cactus—cactus eating sun, sun eating photograph. The sun consumes everything in Arizona, and I figured a little photograph would be gone in no time. I was wrong. The photograph kept going, soaked by rainfall, plastered by mud, pummeled by solar streams. The changes were unremarkable: some curled and frayed edges, banal fading. Photographs made in consumer cameras, developed in commercial labs, are filled with the archivist's assumption: that things should last. That assumption, even more than the golfing ladies, was clear to see.

Shortly after the photograph took its place in the backyard planter, my grandmother began to appear in my dreams with some regularity. Often she's a fantasy version of herself who seems to genuinely like me. She's tender and a little shy when my eyes are closed. For a few months, I dreamed I was with her in a hospital seating area, where she was waiting for my grandfather to die, again. At the time of the dream, both my grandmother and grandfather were already dead. She was calm, perhaps a little resigned. Maybe it was the only scenario in which I could bear to reencounter them. Maybe I was bringing them back to life so I could kill him and force her to watch.

My grandfather, George Miller, was born around 1920 and died sometime around 2001. I'd be more specific, but I don't recall more detail than that. I tried searching for his obituary online but only found my grandmother's. She was born in 1927 and died in 2017. They both struggled to breathe in the end: his lungs taken by war, hers by the finest products of sticky Carolina fields. Those gasping images are my final look at them, images fully imagined since I didn't witness either of their deaths.

There was an order to visiting my grandparents. You entered their Leechburg home through a mudroom that smelled like the garbage compactor it housed. Adults pretended those first steps weren't rank, in the way politeness often forces us to ignore a sense. It smelled like rotting coffee grounds and damp paper plates. The mudroom led to the kitchen, where my grandmother was planted, coffee mug in hand, at the table. The mug held the image of a cardinal in a deep red against a glazed stoneware field. During those early pandemic days, and during some inebriated eBay shopping, I bought two mugs that I thought might be the same as hers. I wanted to drink coffee out of the same mug. My mugs weren't quite the same as hers though. I ended up giving them away.

Back in my grandmother's kitchen, silent waves were exchanged before a short hallway led you into a den-turned-bedroom. That's where my grandfather lived after his stroke, passing indistinguishable hours in an armchair. Only after you greeted him could you speak to my grandmother. Your words went to him first. If you tarried on your way to him, hung out in the kitchen a few extra seconds to chat climate, trouble started.

He'd wheel himself into the kitchen or—for dramatic effect—hoof it with his four-pronged cane. Huff and puff and oxygen hissing from a tube. Coughing. Acting like he might fall down. You'd try to say hi or offer a hand. He'd wave you off.

"You were too busy to come say hi to me when you got here, so don't trouble yourself now."

After he died, my grandmother attempted to pick up the thread. Now it was she who sat in an armchair. When you got to her armchair and said hello, she'd note any detours you took en route and retort:

"I thought you were going to wait 'til it was time to leave to talk to me."

She couldn't quite pull it off. She'd shared in his patriarchal power. She conveyed out to her children and grandchildren each round of abuse he heaped on her. She hit, kicked, sprayed, burned, yelled, cursed, insulted, pulled, dug her painted nails in. After he died, it wasn't the same. When he was around, I really believed their combined anger could bring the roof down on my small body. After he died, she might hit me with a rolled-up magazine, but I had begun to see her bony hands clearly: one gripping the magazine with a tremor and the other bracing her unsteady gait on a table. The patriarch was dead. She was a pretender to a power no one believed in anymore. Nothing was holding her up. When we buried my grandfather, we buried the whole family with him.

Family dissolves, if you didn't know. Maybe you don't want to know, but I wish someone had told me way back then. I thought the close air of the mudroom was forever, but it wasn't. When you bury your family, it opens up space in your life, though buried things can resurface. Each lift of the shovel is a measure of the force at which these memories can come back to me if I dig them back up. While I bury, I find other things. The wood of the shovel handle, the song of metal through dirt, the ache of muscle moving toward desire. There's a symphony inside the wish to forget, not through a refusal to remember but a slow decline in the need to know. One day, I might hear only that symphonic sound and forget the instruments and the composer.

It might seem a little backward, but archivists want to forget too. That's why they laminated all those documents. Lamination was a hope to forget a document for a while, to not have to care for it or worry about its safety. Researchers and day-trippers with sticky fingers and raggedy nails could no longer rip the margins of a love letter from Lord Something to Lady Suchandsuch, not now that plastic had encased the thing. In a way, lamination is a wish to no longer be responsible, to destroy what encumbers you. A good archivist has one key qualification: They don't know that they want to destroy the archives. They dress that want up in a tight commitment to keep and preserve, and you'd never know it wasn't *born like that.*

Michelle Caswell's essay is a fine piece in this style. She argues that the poetic, flimflam way English literature graduate students use the word "archive" to denote any manner of memory thing must be distinguished from the concrete of *actual* archives. Archivists will never get their due if we don't clear things up. It's a practice as old as law: determining what's real and authoritative versus what's dubious, delirious, and fake. It's the old rail against margarine, MSG, and the seedless watermelon. It's the old call against the unnatural and against its malignant spread. If we can't pin down words, lock up molecules, and hush all the clocks, people might start saying "hello" to Gram before Pap, and the whole world will fall apart. The only thing to do is shore up the walls of the actual, concrete archive and empower the true archivists to guard the word. We've got to stop having memories that are false, unproven, and beautiful.

No church chronicle could speak for Holly though. No local website could explain why we want a White Mattock. No video of Snowy could mean what it meant to watch *her as me*. All of that happens on hot breath in a cold minivan, a muddy backwater, a basement fag bar. Trying to save any of that is hopeless. I think the most you can do is recognize you've found a way to burn through time, a way that you hadn't burned before. It'll be different next time, and you'll be pulled into something so deep that you forget your memories and anything that could have prepared you.

Need is an aching sense. Uneconomical. We need what can't be resolved or made useful. For me, one of those needs is water. Deep water. Deep water that does not move. Abandoned, covered in algae, or previously unknown. Sometimes it's real water: lakes, reservoirs. Other times, it's the knowledge that water *was* there.

Not long after the image of Irma went outside, I went online looking for photos of abandoned water parks and the now-defunct SeaWorld Ohio, between Akron and Cleveland. It was a compulsion. Every night, before bed, for weeks, I was—*OK—I have to be really honest about this*

I was horny to look at these photos.

Not genital arousal, but general arousal. I felt *bad* looking at them. Good bad. I felt like someone might catch me. I felt like I was at risk, imperiled. I needed it. More specifically, I needed a whale. An orca.

Free Willy had an outsize impact on me as a child of the 1990s. I wasn't much touched by the orphan story or the Native American uplift, but the whale was a lot. He emerged from the ink of an aquatic park pool. He was the water come to life, reaching up to pull you down, slip you under and through itself. There's the scene where Willy—overtaxed by grubby children demanding his attention—smashes against his tank until the glass cracks and floods the underground viewing chamber.

And then there's the scene that never happened except behind my eyes: the glass quits and water floods the space instantly. Tens of children—including me of wandering eyes—drown in a room that never again knows air. Willy's own body overflows into the viewing chamber and is cut up by the glass. He's a monster dying a leaky death, just slow enough to watch the kids die first. Blood would turn the water orange if light could ever return to the space, but it can't. No one will ever see us again. They'll close down the park and turn off the lights. It's a memory we can't have back.

Of course, the climax of the film-as-made came when Willy was illegally lifted from his tank and transported back to the ocean in a hurried rush against dehydration. Willy was always, it seemed, about to become death—yours or his—in a big way. It was a death that seemed like it could take others out with it, so furious and dominating. And that's the deep pond to me, the lake. The abandoned SeaWorld that absolutely should not have been.

The Ohio orca confirmed my early childhood belief that where I was living had been a prehistoric home to whales. I had evidence. First of all, God did that whole flood-the-earth thing involving Noah, the boat, the rainbow, and Noah having sex with his daughter. I don't know why God did the last part, but I'm explaining the whale and not incest right now. Per my biblically informed understanding of history and marine biology, whales must've swum in and around my hometown during the flood. I used to imagine the whole town bogged down by floodwaters and whales maneuvering between Victorian homes with wraparound porches and marble-facade banks. The whales had even left a record of their visit—a grocery store called "Whalen's."

That was my second piece of evidence. My auditory superstition told me that the way words sounded signaled something about their meaning. If there was a store in town that sounded like "Whale," that must be because a whale used to be there. So if there could have been a whale in my rural Pennsylvania hometown, then it was not so odd that a whale appeared a bit west in suburban Ohio.

But the Whalens whale was here *then*; the Buckeye Shamu was here *now*. Ohio's orca suggested to me that everything old and buried, dead and gone, forgotten but in marks, could be brought back. The sounds of words carried meanings, activated in their sayings. Someone had brought back this whale, and now everyone would cheer and applaud and pay good money to see the past spit on a recent high school graduate in a wetsuit. Nothing is ever over. It's all happening right now.

And it's pulling me down where I'll be touched. By what, I don't know. It's big, though, like the whale. And when it touches me, I will be changed. I want the change and the death, and I want it so much I feel myself losing control and slipping down into the laminating plastic, the whale tank, the pond, the lake.

The first pandemic summer, Harrison and I made trips to Lake Patagonia—about two hours south of Tucson—to escape heat and disease. A manmade dam truncates the Sonoita Creek, which runs through Arizona's Santa Cruz County and turns the water into a destination for boats and picnickers. Early advocates of the lake project admitted that the dam would destroy large tracts of the nearby riparian environment, but the lake would eventually even create more such environment. More good. What's to dislike? The lake's history is very knowable, compared to a lake that predates humans entirely. What came before the lake, what the lake is trying to forget, seems so close to the surface. There could be whole houses at the bottom, like the midflood scenes I imagined outside of Whalen's grocery. There aren't houses at the bottom of Lake Patagonia, but there could be, it's not impossible, and that's what matters here. What isn't seen and can't be seen is so powerfully real. *Something* could be down there. So, it is.

Far from city sounds, I would float on my back atop the creek's surface now broadened into a lake. I had read online that the lake bed drops off steeply, from a few feet of depth to ninety or so. What a terrifying thought: to float atop a fall so great that you'd probably be dead before it finished. I ate it up. I stared up at the uninterrupted blue sky and imagined it to be my lake now. I was floating face down in the sunshine, burning up like Irma Harrison and her unnamed companion.

Her companion's the whole point, isn't she? Irma Harrison was born in New York City in 1909 and died in 2003. For a good portion of her adult life, she lived in Tucson and operated an oil re-refinery with her husband, Myron. The company was called "Amri Oil." Read that backward, though "liO" isn't a word we know just yet. An oil re-refinery takes oil that has already been used and reprocesses it, tries to extract a second consumable life for the product. The place kept catching fire. Irma went out of business. That other woman? She's still in business.

The business of biographies is destroying, then re-creating, mystery. The author tracks down all the relatives, the jobs, the lovers, the lockbox in the storage locker nobody knew about. They get the archivist to crack open the old daybooks and photo albums. They lay the whole life bare

and look at it and what have you got but a flattened chicken for roasting.

There's no more *inside*. Everything's on the surface. All sins confessed, all memories confirmed.

Every good biography soils itself eventually. One or two unanswered questions are posed, even if those questions are unconvincing. For instance, if we know Abraham Lincoln liked pancakes, we find ourselves asking unanswerables like, "Is it because his mother made them or because a pan fell on him as a child?" The question might be interesting in a way, but we're only coming up with it because we want to not know something.

"Nonknowledge." That's the sheering edge of not knowing that writer Georges Bataille chased. In *Accursed Share*, he says that "to know is always to drive, to work; it is always a servile operation, indefinitely resumed, indefinitely repeated."

Knowledge always gets around to being productive, becoming pragmatic. And it's always got a solid object. You know *something*. Bataille wanted to pause on the unknown of the present moment. It's sort of an existentialist claim: in the present moment, we act, and it is in acting (rather than planning or remembering) that we live. Bataille wasn't an existentialist though. It's sort of a surrealist claim: real living is a perpetual "now" with no narrative structure. Everything is flux. The glass of the tank is still breaking and never broken. Bataille was maybe a surrealist at some points, but that's another story. Nonknowledge isn't just not knowing but the point at which knowing is no longer possible.

You, yes, you. Get in the car, because you're driving now. This is Campbell Avenue. It runs north–south in Tucson, six lanes, and we're just hitting the intersection where it meets Grant Street. I don't know why you're driving on this road, why you chose this road, and it's so hot out, and the sun is burning me through the windshield. The sun is almost as loud as the ambulance wail coming up fast behind.

Pull over! No time, no, you can't, no, listen, you can't get to the next block. You've gotta get out of the way. It's life or death. It's the ambulance. It's both. Pull over in the intersection, midintersection, a little bit diagonal, yeah, like that, yeah, all cars facing you.

The ambulance is gone now.

All the lights are turning green again. You're facing southwest, OK, but you're on a north–south road, and everyone is HONKING

What are you DOING? Are you SWEATING? Are you READING A BOOK while you're blocking traffic?

Nonknowledge makes you recognize that you aren't just en route to somewhere or coming from somewhere. You're always already somewhere. And that somewhere, here and now, is so infinitely complex and convoluted that it has the power to pull the air from our lungs—if we let it. And when that happens—when we fall off the swing, hear the car horn blare, see lightning flash close to our faces—what can we do but forget everything?

Remembering is an ethical function nowadays. Good people remember, and the best people remember more, because more memory is more good. People who forget are people who have given up on the promise that we can do things better, prevent evil and horror, by remembering. I understand this promise. Who doesn't? But I don't quite believe it. History is a prosthetic to each human's memory, but despite those long-reaching phalanges, look at what we do. We are still cruel and indifferent. We don't make the future better through memory. We give up on the now to ask about futures we never get around to.

Maybe it's the specter of forgetting that causes us to caricature older women as dotty fools. As we get older and our grip on what has been becomes loose, we're a threat to good society. We can't remember how to be good, can't be reliable witnesses. We forget our own children's childhoods and leave the oven on. We're good life gone rotten. Bataille writes about this too.

In *Eroticism,* he picks a fight with (the already dead) Sigmund Freud about something that's always happening: touching corpses. Freud, per Bataille, had suggested that cultural taboos against touching corpses could be seen as controls against the desire (conscious or unconscious) to touch the dead body of a loved one. Trouble is, nobody's blameless in the unconscious. In a sort of symbolic logic, dead people have taken part in the force that killed them. If that sounds far-fetched, I'll route you back to the story of the Exodus. In these ancient ways of thinking that we still hold in our heads, living or dying is done to you by someone and is somehow deserved. Even "natural deaths" have, at times, been ascribed to the hand of someone somewhere up there.

Bataille countered that very few people really want to touch a dead body, and maybe it's not God we're afraid of anyway. Maybe we're afraid of ourselves and how badly we want corpses to be visions of violence. Elsewhere in Bataille's writing, he tells us that violence is the reason we work. We've sublimated our desire to destroy, clothed it in productive actions. We've taken our primitive need to smash, stab, burn, and created sculpture, cooking, doing surgery. From strangulation to lamination. Sublimation doesn't extinguish desire though. Violence is still there inside us, threatening to destroy not only ourselves but also what we've made through the sublimation of that violence.

But the dead don't work. A corpse produces nothing. It saves nothing. It remembers, keeps account of, nothing. The corpse, and what is a laminated document if not a corpse, is violent and contagious forgetting.

As we age, we get closer and closer to this state. Others sense it, see it, remember it. And so they diminish us. Make us goofy. Give us false teeth and false memories.

Sophia Petrillo had both. A main character on *Golden Girls*, Sophia Petrillo is an octogenarian Sicilian immigrant living in Miami with her daughter, Dorothy, and her roommates, Blanche and Rose. Sophia's backstory includes a stroke that has left her with a fragmented memory and limited impulse control. She blurts out insults for which any other speaker would have to apologize until she's forgotten how to apologize. Sophia gets away with it, because, we're told, she's a *fool* in a way. Her mind has been betrayed by her brain. She's got false teeth too. She washes them in the dishwasher. She remembers beating her dishes on a rock to get them clean. She's domestic chaos. Others, the more lucid around her, fix her "mistakes." To let her ramble is to let her forget wildly, to spread her misremembering into others' good stores of memory. The stroke is a cowardly narrative device, really. She's forgetful, at times confused, but she still knows how to cut and burn. She's fast and bright like hatred—or love, when it's really good.

Think of Sophia the next time StoryCorps comes to town or an archivist asks for your photos. Think of this too:

There's an affinity some of us have to images of older women, characters like Sophia. They've escaped orderly sex. Not the act done to make preachers and presidential candidates, though they're presumed not to do that either. No, they've escaped the expectation that, feeling along their own contours, they will find only one type of texture called "woman." They've already put in their time trying to be a woman. They've aged out of counting as sexual objects, as productive wombs, as nurturing breasts. And how else is a woman to count in America? It's a cruel process, totally indifferent to continuing desires, to all the lingering ambiguities of self-knowledge. Answers have been demanded from them for years, and suddenly no one is listening. And yet, for some of us, some of this seems Edenic: our desires no longer scrutinized, going a little unseen, not mattering in the lineup of boys versus girls, having no reproductive potential, being allowed to be a little out of touch, "eccentric."

What's viciously against these women, what resigns them to the past—that's what it would take for someone like me to live here and now. A position of forgetting. Let me be of no possible use to the household, the church, the archive, the teacher and his revolutions. In this affinity, Sophia and I, we find our linked misery too. We remember, and then are asked to forget, why we want to go unnoticed.

I remember watching Colleen Dewhurst's portrayal of Marilla in the PBS version of *Anne of Green Gables*, when I was around ten. At the time, my eyes so affixed on religious media, I did not understand that the image of Marilla–with her gray hair tied up to get down to work—was a sort of visual meme. It's the Katharine Hepburn type: no nonsense, sturdy fabrics, good posture. The work is exhaustion, expense. It's a woman whose allure is in what she does as much as in how she looks. It's a scene of erotic domination over oneself, and the promise of the transmission of domination.

Marilla worked hard on the farm. I don't quite remember what she did, but she was always a little tired, looking ready for a good sleep. Her strength moved inward and outward. She held herself, faithful to the rigid bones of society. She was a good citizen, a reliable settler. She bruised her soft tissues to hold steady, to hold a bend. And then she would extend it outward, barking a coarse line to pull someone back into the fold, or perhaps to demonstrate some measure of independence, some kind of volition, perhaps the volition that holds her in the order.

I thought Marilla and Helen, my mother's mother, had something in common. They both had tobacco voices. They both seemed nervously friendly to strangers, a touch shy or suspicious. They both could get so coolly angry that you thought they might simply stuff you in a closet and forget about you, lock you away to rot. It wouldn't be a splashy death but a slow, thorough abnegation of your being. It would just be what they felt inside put onto an outside surface.

Helen Dene Knox Swanger Miller was born in Whitwell, Tennessee—a little less than an hour from the Georgia border. Her mother, Nora, died shortly afterward. Her father, Abner, ditched. You might want a story about that, but the truth is that fathers ditch so regularly as to make it unremarkable. Abner ditched. Eugene, my mother's father, ditched. My father ditched. By this third generation, I should be living in a sapphic paradise and calling myself "Wonder Woman." I'm not though.

Raised by her grandfather, whose name might have been Daniel, but I'm fuzzy on these details, Helen stayed in southern Tennessee until her aunt—Ruby?—brought her up to southwestern Pennsylvania. Helen's birthstone was ruby, though, so I might be getting turned around. The aunt kept Helen as a live-in maid until age eighteen. Before she died, Helen's spine had become an inflexible track of scar tissue. A fourth-hand account says it's because of all the beatings from Ruby, or whatever her name was. I wasn't there though. I'm just telling you what made its way to me. We're all collections of what people think they've heard.

Helen lost contact with all her family after she left Ruby, and, perhaps because I was stuck in her family and dreaming of losing contact, and perhaps because I wanted to lose her, I tried to find her family anew. It was the mid-1990s, and Helen had a jazzed-up computer, selected by one of her children and decorated with her crafty sensibilities: a custom mouse pad and a little quilted cover to keep the keyboard from getting dusty. After garbage greetings to Grandpa, I'd kill lonely Sunday afternoons surfing the web. Cousins were rarely around, and I wasn't allowed in rooms occupied by adults. All the grandparents and parents and aunts and uncles would gather to chant, "Children should be seen and not heard." Unspoken addendum: "But they really shouldn't be seen either."

Clicking away on an ergonomic mouse, I began looking for family records on genealogy websites. I prioritized information about Helen's parents, Nora and Abner, and the maybe Daniel. Never Ruby though. She was dead, and we knew too much about her already.

The search results were mixed. I'd find a "Nora Hatfield," but she was born in the wrong year, or her father's name was wrong. More often than not, I'd find someone who seemed like they could be a relative, but the records were so thin that it was hard to tell. Just a vague sense that maybe a connection exists. I fell into this image of my grandmother as a mystery full of dead ends and unknowables. It was so much more of a pleasure than knowing her, the real woman. The unknown of her past hinted at something I wanted and didn't know how to want: a grandmother who was capable of loving me. An image of me being loved.

She's dead in my dreams now. In my dreams, all that's left are plastic bins of photographs. I'm not supposed to have them. I'm taking care of my grandfather. He's alive again. I told you they come back. He has to be held up to walk. His spine is atrophied. He needs odd breathing machines that wander his body at night. When he's sleeping, I go up to her bedroom and look for the bins of photographs so I can return them to my mother. I'm not supposed to. My aunts are on their way, and they'll be angry if I've been in Helen's old room. It's theirs now. Their inheritance.

My grandfather, at first kind, awakes and resumes his cruelty. He accuses me of wanting to put him out with the trash, and I do want this. I pack my belongings, but no one will tell me if I'm doing the right thing. Everyone I try to consult for advice won't talk to me or thinks leaving my family is a step too far. I want so bad to bury them all again, but I don't quite have the courage. I can't hear the shovel singing.

Amanda Lear appears on the television. Amanda Lear, that's another book, is a European disco brilliance, her own enigma. When I first saw a video of her in waking life, I mistook her body for my own. She was beautiful in the way I mean to be beautiful.

In a dreamed television interview, Amanda tells us all that she doesn't like to be thought of as inspiring the new generation. She doesn't like them or what they do. In this dream moment, even the image of the life I mean to live refuses to see me. It says I'm wrong. If that's cruel, it's also the most generous of gifts: nobody's pointing the camera at me anymore. I have to find, have to image, the want inside of myself, by myself, even if it's made of borrowed images—of plants, in photographs, from faggots and women, against God. I have to commit to lamination and its rot.

She isn't singing in the dream, but in waking life, Amanda Lear has this song:

> I'm a photograph.
> I'm a photograph.
> I'm better than the real thing.

A photograph is a kind of sun submerged beneath the waters of a lake.

Some Cameras

Things to try doing, and I mean it:

1. Put a photo of yourself in the sun. Leave it there until you are someone else.
2. Plant plastic roses. Ask your neighbor to water them while you're away.
3. Draw a map of where you live. Put a star where you need an angel to be.
4. Hold your breath until you've found, then lost, a reason to hold your breath.
5. Put a muffin on the ground, then stomp on it. Tell someone the muffin is invasive.
6. Cut one blade of green grass, in the French-cut style, like Julia cuts her beans.
7. Scream underwater. Listen for your echo in the air.
8. Re-create the Miss Pittsburgh 1989 pageant at Pegasus nightclub. Win.
9. Call yourself a faggot, on the phone or otherwise.
10. Ask someone to teach you how to write your name.
11. Pull yourself up by the roots.

Acknowledgments

In the summer of 2021, I emailed Maggie Glover to ask a favor. I'd written a set of essays that I planned to self-publish as a small, cyanotype chapbook. Having always admired Maggie's style, I asked her to give the essays a good editorial going over before I committed it all to paper and sunlight. Maggie responded that she wasn't the person for the job, but she had a friend who might be able to help: Abby Freeland. It's thanks to Maggie's openness, curiosity, and generosity that *Nobody's Psychic* came to be something seeable.

Abby Freeland saw this book before I could. By agreeing to edit this collection, Abby prompted me to take my writing seriously, to ask where it could take me. Abby keeps a space open for art—an impossible task in this world. My endless gratitude to Abby and everyone at the University Press of Kentucky.

Also impossible, in the very best way, in the Bataillean sense: my mahjong friends. Each Sunday, before the week's writing and editing began, a group of friends met at our home to play mahjong. Their humor, kindness, and encouragement made it possible for me to sustain this work. In this book, I imagine talking to each and every one of you: Andrew Dunn, Cole Eskridge, Jesse Factor, Jason Gates, Marcy Held, John Musser, and Larry Shea.

During my time in Arizona, Eva Hayward kept me curious about where language could and couldn't go: impossibilities against apathy. Her wit and acumen are irreplaceable. On a messy Mother's Day in 2021, Rachel Wedig sat across from me at a Tucson gay bar and asked, "So when are you writing a book?" The question wasn't rhetorical. Thank you, Rachel.

Over the past few years, I've been fortunate to share excerpts from this collection in readings and performances. Thank you to Alicia Kozma at the Indiana University Cinema and Anya

Clarke-Verdery and Mitsuko Clarke-Verdery at *inter-*, in Pittsburgh, for hosting me. Thank you to Ky Brown and Kate Palmer-Albers, as well, for providing smart and encouraging feedback on essays in this collection. My special appreciation to Joan for hearing me and helping me hear myself.

Many hours were spent reading, editing, and researching at the Carnegie Libraries of Pittsburgh. The librarians and archivists there, especially Kelsea Collins, offered invaluable assistance. Tom McCaffrey and Tim Cheney of The Edge Hill Rounders kindly allowed me to share lyrics from their song "Die! Die! Die! Spotted Lanternfly."

When the time came to arrange for an author photo, I was relieved to know that Centa Schumacher is in this world. Centa's photography keeps faith with the multiple, the multiplied, and the imagined. Thank you to Centa for making an image with, rather than against, me.

Finally, thank you to Harrison Apple. I would talk about you more in these pages, but you tell your own story so exquisitely through how you live your life. I learn so much from you. And so, this book is for Harrison, who remains better than the real thing.

Further Reading

Bataille, Georges. *Visions of Excess: Selected Writings, 1927–1939*. Edited by Allan Stoekl. Translated by Allan Stoekl, with Carl R. Lovitt and Donald M. Leslie Jr. Minneapolis: University of Minnesota Press, 1985.

Caswell, Michelle. "'The Archive' Is Not an Archives: On Acknowledging the Intellectual Contributions of Archival Studies." *Reconstruction: Studies in Contemporary Culture* 16, no. 1 (2016). http://reconstruction.digitalodu.com/Issues/161/Caswell.shtml.

Chalker-Scott, Linda. *How Plants Work: The Science behind the Amazing Things Plants Do*. Portland, OR: Timber Press, 2015.

Deloria, Philip. *Playing Indian*. New Haven, CT: Yale University Press, 1998.

Ferrence, Matthew. *Appalachia North: A Memoir*. Morgantown: West Virginia University Press, 2019.

Freud, Sigmund. *The Psychopathology of Everyday Life*. Edited by James Strachey. Translated by Alan Tyson. New York: W. W. Norton, 1965.

Guilbert, Hervé. *Ghost Image*. Translated by Robert Bononno. Chicago: University of Chicago Press, 2014.

Hayward, Eva. "Fingeryeyes: Impressions of Cup Corals." *Cultural Anthropology* 25, no. 4 (2010): 577–599.

Hayward, Eva. "Painted Camera, 'Her.'" *e-flux Journal* 117 (April 2021). https://www.e-flux.com/journal/117/385172/painted-camera-her.

Lepselter, Susan. *The Resonance of Unseen Things: Poetics, Power, Captivity, and UFOs in the American Uncanny*. Ann Arbor: University of Michigan Press, 2016.

Marder, Michael. *Plant-Thinking: A Philosophy of Vegetal Life.* New York: Columbia University Press, 2013.

Mosher, Ann. *Capital's Utopia: Vandergrift, Pennsylvania, 1855–1916.* Baltimore: Johns Hopkins University Press, 2004.

Obermeyer, Brice. *Delaware Tribe in a Cherokee Nation.* Lincoln: University of Nebraska Press, 2009.

Ono, Yoko. *Grapefruit: A Book of Instruction and Drawings.* New York: Simon & Schuster, 1970.

Steedman, Carolyn Kay. *Landscape for a Good Woman: A Story of Two Lives.* New Brunswick, NJ: Rutgers University Press, 1987.

Woodward, Eddie. "The Epidemic in the Archives: A Layman's Guide to Cellulose Acetate Lamination." *RBM: A Journal of Rare Books, Manuscripts, and Cultural Heritage 18*, no. 2 (2017): 108-122.

About the Author

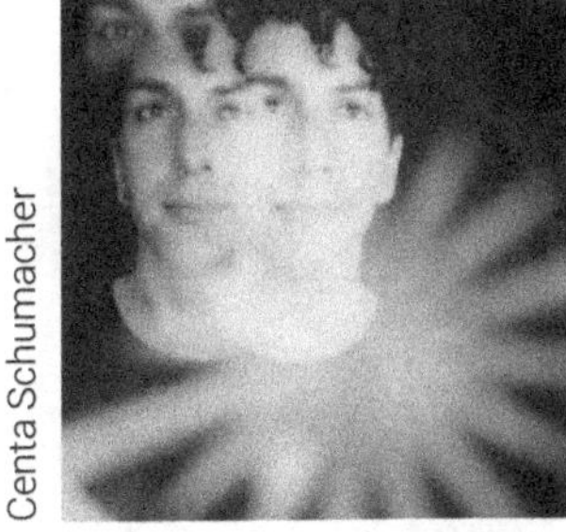

Centa Schumacher

Dani Lamorte is a Pittsburgh-based artist who writes, performs, and makes photographic images. Their work has appeared in *Observer*, the *Cleveland Review of Books*, the *Pittsburgh City Paper*, and *100 Days in Appalachia*, among other publications.

APPALACHIAN FUTURES
Black, Native, and Queer Voices

SERIES EDITORS: Annette Saunooke Clapsaddle, Davis Shoulders, and Crystal Wilkinson

This book series gives voice to Black, Native, Latinx, Asian, Queer, and other nonwhite or ignored identities within the Appalachian region.

Black Freedom Struggle in Urban Appalachia
Edited by J. Z. Bennett, Christy L. McGuire, Lori Delale-O'Connor, T. Elon Dancy II, and Sabina Vaught

Affrilachia: Testimonies
Chris Aluka Berry with Kelly Elaine Navies and Maia A. Surdam

No Son of Mine: A Memoir
Jonathan Corcoran

To Belong Here: A New Generation of Queer, Trans, and Two-Spirit Appalachian Writers
Edited by Rae Garringer

Tar Hollow Trans: Essays
Stacy Jane Grover

Nobody's Psychic: Finding & Losing Yourself
Dani Lamorte

Deviant Hollers: Queering Appalachian Ecologies for a Sustainable Future
Edited by Zane McNeill and Rebecca Scott

Reading, Writing, and Queer Survival: Affects, Matterings, and Literacies across Appalachia
Caleb Pendygraft

Queer Communion: Religion in Appalachia
Davis Shoulders, with a foreword by Willie Edward Taylor Carver Jr.

Appalachian Ghost: A Photographic Reimagining of the Hawk's Nest Tunnel Disaster
Raymond Thompson Jr.